AF540826

Dictionary of Bhagavad Gita

Dictionary of Bhagavad Gita

Compiled with an Introduction
by
Dr. Bibekananda Banerjee

Kaveri Books
New Delhi - 110 002

First Published in 2018
ISBN : 978-93-86463-09-8

Published by
Kaveri Books
4832/24, Ansari Road,
Daryaganj, New Delhi - 110 002 (India)
Ph. : 011-47072321
E-mail : kaveribooks@gmail.com
Website : www.kaveribooks.com

Typesetting at Creative Graphics, Delhi

PRINTED IN INDIA

INTRODUCTION

The Gita is recognized as a philosophical work all over the world. This was written in Sanskrit language and available in *Bhismaparva* of the *Mahabharata*, compiled by Vedavyasa. The Mahabharata is known as National Epic of India. The Gita consists of only eighteen chapters of the Bhismaparva (25-42). Each chapter of the Gita represents the different yogas or method of knowledge of practical life as well as spiritual wisdom.

The first chapter of the popular work describes the detailed picture of battle field of Kuruksetra. Both the armies of Kaurava and Pandava met with for fighting against each other.

"dharmakṣetre kurukṣetre samaveta yuyutsavaḥ I 1.1

The blind king Dhrtarastra, father of Duryodhana asked Sanjaya, what to be done by our armies and what part will be played in the field of Kuruksetra.

The answer was given by Sanjaya accordingly and the subject-matter of Gita starts. At the very beginning an unexpected event happened in the battle field. The third brother of Pandava, Arjuna is in deep overwhelmed and Lord Krsna tries to give impetus to overcome the sorrows of him.

Arjuna was not ready to fight against Kaurava as his relatives and left all the weapons out of depression.

evamuktvārjuna saṁkhye rathopastha upavīśat I
viṣrjya saśaraṁ cāpaṁ śokasaṁvignāmanasaḥ II1.47

This is known as *'Arjunavisadayoga'* the first chapter of the Gita. Lord Krsna continuously taught Arjuna the spiritual knowledge to come out from depression. He told Arjuna, you are neither master nor creator of anything in this universe. You will not be able to kill anybody. They are already killed. He also told, you are fully covered by *Ajnana* (ignorance), you first be free from *Ajnana* and acquire the metaphysical knowledge, by which you can free yourself from earthly attachments.

You should have unheld the similar state of mind at pleasure and sorrow, profit and loss, victory and defeat, and fight as your own duty.

You should have made yourself immobile mental status, (*sthitaprajna*). Then you will be free from every bondage, every passion, every conflict and every paradigms in your life at every moment.

Lord Krsna taught Arjuna, in the second chapter, the symptoms of man to attend acquiring real knowledge about God. At the end of the second chapter he told to Arjuna, he who has been free from all desires, affection, egotism of life he can only attend the spiritual knowledge.

Then we come into the third chapter of the Gita where Lord Krsna gives the lesson regarding *Karma* (work). Here Arjuna liked to know about the role of *Karma* in human life. Arjuna was taught by Krsna that knowledge is superior to *Karma*, he also asked Krsna if it is true, why you introduce me to *Karma* again?

The answer comes from Krsna, that nobody can live a moment without *Karma* and this is a process of human life. Without work the body will be destroyed. But the question is what type of work you should do, and what type of return you like to have behind the work. The answer is you should perform that type of *Karma* which are recognized by the *Sastras*, side by side you should leave any type of wanting, and you should not want the result of the work which you have done.

tyktvā karmaphalāsaṅgaṁ nityatrpto nirāśrayaḥ I 4.20

At the end of the third chapter Lord Krsna advised Arjuna, you should remember that human sense-organ is superior to earthly body, mind is superior to sense-organ, intelligence is superior to mind, and *Atma* (soul) is superior to intelligence, you should acquire the above perfect knowledge and fight against the enemies.

In the fourth chapter again we see that Lord Krsna described the qualities of perfect knowledge to Arjuna. He also advised Arjuna, you learn the perfect knowledge from your *Acarya* (Teacher), by faith, and faithful performance only. You should sacrifice the results all of your works to another.

na māṁ karmāṇi limpanti na me karmaphale spṛḥa I

iti māṁ yobhijānāti karmabirna sa vadhyate I I 4.14

Last of all, this is my advise that you always do your work with asceticism, determination and devotion by which you will attend with perfect knowledge.

The fifth chapter of the Gita is known as '*Karmasnnyasayoga*'. Here Arjuna asked Lord Krsna, which one will acquire by me either *Karmasannyasa* or *Karmayoga*, and which one will better for me. Lord Krsna said to Arjuna, the *sannyasa* and yoga are not different, ultimately these are same.

yuktaḥ karmaphalam tyaktvā śāntimāpnoti naiṣṭḥkīm I

ayukta kāmakāreṇa phale sakto nivadhyate I I 5.12

The meaning of the yoga is self-restrain with intense concentration. He who liked to control himself, he must have yoga by his spirit. He will be happy who can able to control his mind. So man is a friend of his own, side by side he is the enemy of his own.

In the sixth chapter of the Gita Lord Krsna explained the *Dhyanayoga* or *Atmasamyamayoga* to Arjuna. Here he says to Arjuna he who will not be able to leave desires, he will not be a *Yogi*. Everyone will see me like *Atma* in everything as well as everything are with me. He who will always recollect me with faith he will be the best yogi among all. So Arjuna, you should make yourself as *Yuktotama* and he who is *Yuktatama* he is *madgatenantaratmana* by his devotion. He will open a new door in the world.

When we open the seventh chapter of the Gita, we see Arjuna liked to have the knowledge of his profit from Lord Krsna. Krsna told Arjuna, that everything was created from inanimation and consciousness. And I am the primary cause of the creation and destruction. I am also the basic cause of all Gods. I stay in my devotees heart and always enlighten them. I know past, present and future, but the man who has no faith can not be able to know me.

All the living beings are hypnotized by illusion and three *Gunas*. I am only beyond the three *Gunas* and I am imperishable. The devotee he who is always attached with me, he will be the best wise. The wise can be able to know me ultimately after his death. He can see me through crossing the bar of darkness of death.

In the eighth chapter Lord Krsna advised to Arjuna the '*Aksarabrahmayoga*' and taught him everything is changeable, destructive, revolving except '*Brahma*'. Only realizing '*Aksara-brahma*' one can overcome the rebirth and free from earthly mortality.

Lord Krsna told Arjuna the *Rajavidya* or *Rajaguhyavidya* in the ninth chapter of the Gita. The real teaching of Lord Krsna of this chapter is, though I am in the creation but I am the outside of the creation (*srsti*).

'matsthāni sarvabhūtani na cāham teṣvavavasthitaḥ' | 9.4

In the tenth chapter of the Gita Lord Krsna explained his enlightenment to Arjuna. He also said which is the greatest, finest and best thing in the world. I stay in such beautiful thing. So that this chapter is known as '*Vibhutiyoga*'

nāntosti mama divyānāṁ vibhūtīnāṁ parantapa | 10.40

In the eleventh chapter we see, Arjuna liked to see the real form of Lord Krsna.

'draṣṭumicchāmi te rūpamaiśvaram puruṣottama' | 11.3

After heard the Arjunas prayer Krsna gave him the power of his eyes by that Arjuna will be able to see the form that is known as '*Visvarupa*' (divine form) of Lord Krsna.

Arjuna visualized that He is the creator in one hand and destroyer in another. He stated the universe as time. Arjuna did not able to see the terrible form of Lord Krsna, he overwhelmed with fear and liked to see the peaceful form of Krsna. According to Kathopanisad –

yadidam kiñca jagat sarvam prāṇa ejati nihsṛtam |

Lord Krsna advised the awakening to Arjuna after showing his divine form. At a moment Krsna showed the real doctrine of the earthly world itself.

The subject-matter of Gita may be come to an end here but Arjuna wanted to know how he can get the blessing of Almighty. So Lord Krsna told him regarding devotion and by that one can meet immortality. If a devotee will give his mind, intelligent, to him he can live in his Lord. He is the greatest devotee who can be able to see Him in all the creation of the world.

Not only that a real devotee will feel the same mental position in pleasure and sorrow, enemies and friends, honour and dishonor, in cold and hot.

Here, in the Bhaktiyoga, in the twelvth chapter Lord Krsna explains the qualities of real Devotee (*Bhakta*) one by one.

yona hṛṣyati na dveṣṭi na śocati na kāṅksati |
śubhāśubhaparityāgī bhaktiman yaḥ sa me priyaḥ || 12.17

The thirteenth chapter of the Gita is known as '*Ksetraksetrajnavibhagayoga*'. Here Lord Krsna wanted to explain the nature of *Ksetra* and *Ksetrajna* clearly. He told to Arjuna, the human body is always *Ksetra*, because it is a piece of land of cultivation of thoughts. If we cultivate the seed in the land after certain time it will give us fruits. As like as the human body which will do something by his mind and body with own habits the result will be appeared to him timely.

Lord Krsna also told Arjuna, who can be able to know this nature of human body, the wise called him *Ksetranjna*.

I am the *Ksetrajna* (*Jivatma*) of all the *Ksetras* and who clearly knows the difference between *Ksetra* and *Ksetrajna* including changeable *Ksetra* (*Prakrti*) and *Ksetrajna* (unchangeable *Purusa*), and that is real knowledge.

Ksetrajñancāpi mām biddhi sarvakṣetreṣu bhārata |
kṣetra kṣetrajñayorjnānam yattaj jñānam matam mama ||
13.2

Who can be able to see and realize God is in everybody and in everything; he will really acquire perfect knowledge or spiritual knowledge that is always different from ignorance (*ajnana*).

By that knowledge one can be able to know the unchangeable things and changeable things in the materialistic world.

The *Paramatma* (Sureme Being) is in everywhere so wise can realize it in very near but the man who is full of ignorance can realize it is very far from him.

So, who can be able to realize the difference between *Ksetra* and *Ksetrajna* and try to free from changeable *Prakrti* and its action by spiritual knowledge, he can meet *Paramatma* (Supreme Being).

Then we come to the fourteenth chapter of the Gita where Lord Krsna explained Arjuna about three *Gunas*, that this chapter is known as *Gunatrayvibhagayoga*.

Krsna told Arjuna, *Sattva*, *Raja* and *Tama*, these three *Gunas* are created from *Prakrti* (nature). And these three Gunas surrounded the soul.

Sattvaṁ rajastama iti gunāh prakrtisambhavā |
nibadhanti mahāvaho dehe dehinamavyayam || 14.5

Out of three Gunas, the Sattva is very fair, manifested and unchangeable, by this *Guna Jivatma* make its barrier by ego and feel that he is happy, wise etc.

The second *Guna* named *Raja* is full of passion and it creates desire and attachment and binds the *Jivatma* by *Karma* (work).

And the third *Tama* by name, which creates from *Ajnana* (ignorance). It always binds the man by distress, lethargy and sleep.

The result of the *Rajasika* work is sorrow and the result of the *Tamasika* work is *Ajnana* (ignorance).

The man who can be able to overcome the above three *Gunas*, he can cross the birth, with joy.

Then the fifteenth chapter of Gita started. The name of this chapter is '*Purusottamayoga*'. This chapter is completed in twenty verses only.

Lord Krsna told Arjuna, if you like to know me, you realize me as a whole. I have already told you about my three different forms. One of my form is *Ksara* and second one is the form of *Aksara* with explain the form of *Ksetrajna* and now I told you about my form and nature of *Purusottama*.

yasmāt kṣaramatītohamakṣarādapi cottamaḥ ।
atosmi loke vade ca prathitaḥ puruṣottamaḥ ।।18

You should know me having three forms. One of my form is always changing, it is one of the condition of consciousness, and second one is unchangeable form of consciousness and the third one is the form of my *Purusottama* by name. I told the above two forms by the form of *Purusottama* who knows me having the said condition he can be able to know everything. Here end the *Purusottamayoga* chapter.

The Gita was at end after describing the *Purusottamayoga*, but Lord Krsna liked to inform Arjuna at the highest stage of the platform where he can stay forever.

Krsna actually wanted salvation of Arjuna. He advised Arjuna, about three *Gunas*. Not only that if one wants to overcome the *Gunas*, he should obtain *Daivisampad* and reduce the *Asurisampad*.

Vanity, pride, self-respect, passion, cruelty and ignorance these all are the signs of man belonged *Asurisampad*.

On the other hand the man who obtains the qualities like, sacrifice, surrender, kindness, tolerance and purity he may be identified as a man of having *Daivisampad*.

The man who can obtain the qualities of *Daivisampad*, he can easily get *Nirvana* or salvation.

The seventeenth chapter of the Gita is '*Sraddhatrayavibhagayoga*' by name. In this chapter Lord Krsna gave the vivid description are *Sraddha* (respect). Three types of *Sraddha* are *Sattviki*, *Rajasi* and *Tamasi*.

Every man must have the quality of *Sraddha* (respect). *Sraddha* (respect) controls the man. In Yoga Philosophy without *Sraddha* (respect) nobody can attend salvation.

We also see in the *Kathopanisad*, that Naciketa attended to the knowledge of self-consciousness by *Sraddha* (respect).

Śraddhā aviveśa

Now we come to the eighteenth chapter of the Gita named '*Moksayoga*'. This is the last chapter of the Gita. Salvation is the main wanting of human being. Without knowing himself nobody can attend salvation. And only knowledge can free a man from birth and death. Gita is the essence of the Upanisad. Lord Krsna was the inspirer of spiritual knowledge to Arjuna. All the learned persons and the listeners are enjoyers of the spiritual thoughts like as nectar.

sarvopaniṣado gāvo dogdhā gopālanandanaḥ |
pārtho vatsaṁ sudhīrbhoktā dugdhaṁ gītāmṛtaṁ mahat ||

The Gita was started with sadness and it ends with pleasure. So the Gita teaches us, gradually a man can get better mental sphere by his own efforts towards salvation by good works and spiritual thoughts.

In this context we may consider few words of Charles Wilkins about the Gita. "The Gita a performance of great originality of a sublimity of conception, reasoning and diction, almost unequalled and a single exception among all the known religious mankind" etc.

The Bhagavad Gita (Song of God) is one of the most revered sacred scriptures of Hinduism and is considered as one of the most important religious classics of the world. This *Dictionary of Bhagavad Gita* comprises of transliteration, English meaning of the each Sanskrit words of the verses of the Gita and chapter index of almost every word from all eighteen chapters of Gita, arranged alphabetically. The doubtful Sanskrit words are also given the meaning by lucid English version.

This excellent work in a meaningful manner will come in very handy for a beginner who likes to study and understand the meaning of the verses of the Gita and will be of interest to the students, researchers in this subject with a great interest and love.

Bibekananda Banerjee

Dictionary of Bhagavad Gita

Sanskrit Word	Ch.	Slok	Meaning
aacharah	16	7	good behaviour
aacharan	3	19	doing
aacharatah	4	23	undertaken
aacharati	3	21	does
aacharya	1	3	teacher
aadarsah	3	38	a mirror
aadau	3	41	after first
aadhatsva	12	8	fix
aadhyah	16	15	wealthy
aadyantavantah	5	22	having a beginning and an end
aadih	10	2	the source
aadim	11	16	beginning
aadityan	11	6	The group of Sun gods.They are twelve in number
aajyam	9	16	Ghee melted and clarified for offering in the sacrifice. oblation
aakasam	13	32	space
aakasa-sthitah	9	6	situated in space
aakhyahi	11	31	tell
aakhyatam	18	63	imparted
aarambhah	14	12	undertaking
aarjavam	13	7	sincerity

Sanskrit Word	Ch.	Slok	Meaning
aartah	7	16	one who is in peril
aaruruksoh	6	3	for one who aspires to ascend
aasadhya	9	2	having reached
aasanam	6	11	seat
aasane	6	12	on the seat
aascharyani	11	6	wonders
aashaa-paasha-shataih	16	12	bound by hundreds of hopes
aashayaat	15	8	from seats
aasinah	14	23	sitting
aasinam	9	9	remaining
aasita	2	54	should sit
aasrayet	1	36	accrue
aasritah	12	11	resorted to
aasritam	9	11	who have taken
aaste	3	6	sits
aasthaya	7	2	adopting
aasurah	16	7	related to the non-divine beings
aasuram	7	15	demoniacal
aasuri	16	5	demoniacal nature
aatataayinah	1	36	criminals - One who sets fire to the house of, administers poison to, steals the wealth, land, and wife of, another person

Sanskrit Word	Ch.	Slok	Meaning
aatma	6	5	Self. Gita-verses 11-30 in Chapter II and again in Verses 5 and 6 in VI. Atma is eternal, all pervading, immovable and immutable
aatma-bhava sthah	10	11	situated in their hearts
aatma-yogat	3	13	through the power of My yoga (see under Yoga)
aavartate	8	26	he returns
aavartinah	8	16	liable to return
aavesita-chetasam	12	7	who have their minds fixed on
aavesya	8	1	having fixed
aavriyate	3	38	is surrounded
aavrtya	3	4	having covered
abhaktaya	18	67	to one who lacks devotion
abhibhavati	1	4	overtakes
abhibuya	14	1	prevails
abhidhasyati	18	68	will speak of
abhihita	2	39	has been conveyed
abhijananti	9	24	they know
abhi-janavan	16	15	of noble birth
abhijayate	13	1	arises
abhimukhah	11	2	towards
abhinandati	1	4	welcomes
abhipravrittah	4	2	engaged in action
abhisandhaya	17	12	in expectation
abhi-vijvalanti	11	28	blazing

Sanskrit Word	Ch.	Slok	Meaning
abhyadhikah	11	43	greater
abhyanunadyan	1	19	resounding
abhyarchya	18	46	by worshipping
abhyasath	12	12	practise
abhyasa-yoga yuktena	8	8	involved in the yoga of practice
abhyasa-yogena	12	9	through the yoga of practice
abhyasuyakah	16	18	jealous by nature
abhyasuyantah	3	32	criticising
abhyasuyati	18	67	speaks ill
achala-pratistham	2	7	permenant and beyond change; imperishable, well established
acharam	13	15	moving
achintyam	12	3	inconceivable
achintyarupam	8	9	whose form is inconceivable
achyuta	1	21	name of Vishnu - Krishna
adambhitvam	13	7	devoid of deceit
adbhutam	11	2	amazing
adesakale	17	22	at an improper place and time
adhah-sakham	15	1	whose branches spread downwards
adhamam	16	2	lower
adharmabhibhavat	1	41	when adharma dominates
adharmam	18	31	sin; opposite of dharma

Sanskrit Word	Ch.	Slok	Meaning
adhibhutam	8	1	the level of creation from where the five basic elements of ether, air, fire, water and earth are active
adhidaivam	8	1	the level of creation from where the divinity and the gods are active
adhidaivatam	8	4	the entity in the divine plane
adhigacchati	2	64	attains
adhipatyam	2	8	sovereignty
adhisthanam	3	4	dwelling place
adhiyajnah	8	2	the level of the activity from where the effects of the sacrifice starts
adhruvam	17	18	temporary
adhyaks ena	9	1	as the overseer
adhyatma chetasa	3	3	with concentration on the self steadiness in the knowledge of
adhyatma-jn'ana nityatvam	13	11	the spirit
adhyesyate	18	7	those who study this
adrohah	16	3	absence of enmity
adrsta-purvam	11	45	not seen before
adya	4	3	today
agama-apayinah	2	14	have a beginning and an end
agatasun	2	11	those whoare still living
agham	3	13	sin

Sanskrit Word	Ch.	Slok	Meaning
aghayuh	3	16	a person who leads a sinful life
agnih	4	37	god of fire
agre	18	37	in front of
aha	1	2	said
ahah	8	17	day
a-haitukam	18	22	illogical
aharah	17	7	food
ahave	1	31	in battle
ahimsa	10	5	The principle of not harming or hurting anybody or anything. This is a fundamental tenet of Hinduism, Buddhism and Jainism
ahitah	2	36	harmful
aho	1	45	alas
aho	17	1	oh
ahoratra- vidah	8	17	those who know about day and night
ahuh	3	42	say
aisvaram	9	5	belonging to divinity
ajah	2	2	One who is not born; meaning thereby permenant, transcendent
ajasram	16	19	for all time
ajnana	11	41	not knowing
ajnanajam	10	11	arising from ignorance
ajnana-vimohitah	16	15	deluded by ignorance

Sanskrit Word	Ch.	Slok	Meaning
akarma	4	16	inaction meaning therby absence of a specific type of action; technically inaction is also a type of action
akartaram	4	13	non-performer
aksara samud-bhavam	3	15	the transcendent as the origin; that which does not die
aksaranam	10	33	of the letters
aksayah	10	33	endless
akusalam	18	1	Action which ends up with unworthy result; not safe
alasah	18	28	lazy
aloluptvam	16	2	freedom from covetousness
alpa-buddhyah	16	93	of small intellect
alpam	18	22	trivial
alpa-medhasam	7	23	who are of little wisdom
amalan	14	14	flawless
amanitvam	13	7	modesty
ami	11	21	these
amrtatvaya	2	15	for immorality
amsah	15	7	a part
amsuman	10	21	the radiant
anabhisvangah	13	9	absence of affection
anadim	10	3	without beginning
anadi-madhya	11	19	without beginning, middle and end
anadimat	13	12	devoid of beginning
anahamvadi	18	26	not egoistic

Sanskrit Word	Ch.	Slok	Meaning
anahankarah	13	8	free from egoistic attitude
analah	7	4	fire
anamayam	2	51	beyond all evils
ananta	11	37	0, infinite
ananta-bahum	11	19	having enormous arms
anantam	11	11	endless
anantavirya	11	19	having enormous energy
ananyena	12	6	single-minded
anarambhat	3	4	by not commencing
anaryajushtam	2	2	unworthy of a refined cultured person following the sanatana dharma
anasnatah	6	16	for one who does not eat
anas'ritah	6	1	without reliance on
anasuyantah	3	31	without the feeling of jealousy
anatmanah	6	6	for one who has not disciplined oneself
anavalokayan	6	13	not seeing
anavrttim	8	23	having no re-birth
anekadha	11	13	differently
anena	3	1	by this
angani	2	58	limbs
anicchan	3	36	against his desire
aniketah	12	19	one who has no home
anirdesyam	12	3	the indefinable
anistam	18	12	unpleasant
anityah	2	14	ephemeral

Sanskrit Word	Ch.	Slok	Meaning
anityam	9	33	fleeting
anna-sambhavah	3	14	born out of food
anoh	8	9	than the subtle
antam	11	16	end
antar-aramah	5	24	has inner joy
antaratmana	6	47	with his mind
antare	5	27	between
antavantah	2	18	perishable
antavat	7	23	limited
ante	7	19	at the end
antike	13	15	near
anu dvegakaram	17	15	painless
anusmaret	8	9	thinking on
anya-devata bhaktah	9	23	worshippers of other deities
anyam	7	5	the other
anyani	2	22	other
anyatha	13	11	other
anyatra	3	9	other than
apaisunam	16	2	aversion to vilification
apalayanam	18	43	not withdrawing
apanam	4	29	incoming breath. Refers to the energy with which food, solid and liquid, not absorbed into the body, is carried downward. It is the compliment of Pranic force
apane	4	29	in the incoming breath

Sanskrit Word	Ch.	Slok	Meaning
apara	7	5	lower
aparajitah	1	17	unconquerable
aparam	4	4	later
aparan	16	14	other
aparani	2	22	other
apare	4	25	other
apariharye	2	27	over'what is unavoidable
aparimeyam	16	11	numerous
aparyaptam	1	1	unlimited
apatrebhyah	17	22	to the undeserving
apavrtam	2	32	open
apohanam	15	5	lose
aprameyam	11	17	without limit
apravrttih	4	13	inactivity
apunaravrittim	5	17	the state of non returning
architum	7	21	to worship
arhah	1	37	justified
arhati	2	17	is able
arpita-mano buddhih	8	7	by devoting mind and intellect
artha vyapasrayah	3	18	dependence on any object
arthaka man	2	5	greedy for riches
asamshayam	6	35	doubtless
asasvatam	8	15	temporary
asat	9	19	non-existence
asesatah	6	24	completely
asesena	4	35	without exception

Sanskrit Word	Ch.	Slok	Meaning
Asita	10	13	father of the sage Devala
asnute	3	4	attain
asrada-dhanah	9	3	without faith
astikyam	18	42	belief that god exists
asusrusave	18	67	to one who does no service
atandritah	3	23	free from laziness and sleep; energetically
atapaskaya	18	67	to one who has not
austerities			performed
atatvarthavat	18	22	unconcerned with truth
athava	6	42	or
ati-adbhutam	18	77	highly mysterious and wonderful
atimanita	16	3	haughtiness
atindriyam	6	21	beyond the perception of senses transcendent and divine
atistha	4	4	undertake
ati-svapna-silasya	6	16	one who is prone to sleep and dreaming beyond limits
atitaranti	13	25	overcome
atitya	14	2	having gone beyond
ativa	12	2	very
ativartate	6	44	transcends
atma aupamyena	6	32	criteria one would apply to one
atma-suddhayae	5	11	for purifying the heart
atma-vibhutayah	10	1	of your own manifestations
atma-visuddhaye	6	12	for purifying self

Sanskrit Word	Ch.	Slok	Meaning
atyaginam	18	12	to those who do not practise charity and sacrifice
atyantam	6	28	supreme
atyartham	7	17	very much
atyasnatah	6	16	for one who eats in excess
avachya vadan	2	36	indecent words
avadhyah	2	3	can never be killed
avagaccha	10	41	know
avahasa artham	11	42	in fun
avajnatam	17	12	with insult
avapasyasi	2	33	you will commit
avapnoti	15	8	obtains
avapsyatha	3	11	you shall achieve
avaptavyam	3	22	to be obtained
avaptum	6	36	to obtain
avapya	2	8	having obtained
avapyate	12	5	achieved
avaram	2	49	inferior
avasadayeth	6	5	denigrate
avasah	3	5	under pressure
avasam	9	8	powerless
avasisyate	7	2	there remains
avastabhya	9	8	holding under control
avasthatum	1	3	to stand
avasthitah	9	4	arrayed
avasthitam	15	11	existing

Sanskrit Word	Ch.	Slok	Meaning
avatisthati	14	23	acts
avibhaktam	13	16	undivided
avijneyam	13	15	incomprehensible
avikampena	10	7	unfaltering
avikaryah	2	25	unalterable
avinasdyantam	13	27	indestructible
avyabhicharena	14	26	through the unwavering
avyabhicharini	13	1	unfaltering
avyabhicharinya	18	37	which is unfailing
avyakta-murtina	9	4	in My unmanifested form
avyaktat	12	5	from the unmanifested
avyavatma	4	6	of nature
avyayam	2	21	imperishable
avyayasya	2	17	of that which is immutable
ayanesu	1	11	in the divisions of the army
ayashah	10	5	infamy
ayatha vat	18	31	incorrectly
ayatih	6	37	not energetic
ayuktasya	2	66	for one who lacks concentration
baalaah	5	4	children
baddhah	16	12	bound
badhnati	14	6	it binds
badhyate	4	14	becomes bound
bahavah	1	9	many
bahih	5	27	outside

Sanskrit Word	Ch.	Slok	Meaning
bahu damstra - karalam	11	23	terrible with many teeth
bahu-baahu-uru padam	11	23	having many arms, thighs and feet. The reference is to the cosmic vision of the lord
bahudha	9	15	variously
bahula-ayssam	18	24	very strenuous
bahumatah	2	35	acceptable
bahuna	10	42	elaborately
bahunam	7	19	of many
bahu-shakaah	2	41	with many branches
bahu-udaram	11	23	the reference is to the cosmic form of the lord; with many bellies
bahu-vidhah	4	32	various kinds
bahya-sparsesu	5	21	the touch; external; external objects
balam	1	1	strength
balavan	16	14	man of strength
balavatam	7	11	of the strong
bandham	18	3	bondage
bandhuh	6	5	relative, friend
bhaavesu	10	17	in moods
bhah	11	12	radiance
bhaiksyam	2	5	on alms
bhajatam	10	1	those who worship
bhaktah	4	3	devotee
bhaktiman	12	1	who is wholly devoted

Sanskrit Word	Ch.	Slok	Meaning
bhakti-yogena	14	26	by the yoga of devotion
bhakty upahratam	9	26	presented with devotion
Bharata	1	24	scion of Bharata dynasty
Bharatarsabha	3	41	Best of Bharatas; name of Arjuna
Bharata-sattama	18	4	name of Arjuna
Bharata-srestha	17	12	name of Arjuna
bhartaa	9	16	supporter
bhasa	2	54	description
bhasah	11	12	radiance
bhasase	2	11	you speak
bhasayate	15	6	illumines
bhasmasat	4	37	to ashes
bhasvata	10	11	with the radiant lamp of knowledge
bhava	2	45	fixed
bhava-samanvitah	10	8	full of fervour
bhava-samsuddhih	17	16	the purity of heart
bhavah	10	4	existence
bhavah	2	16	being
bhavaih	7	13	by nature
bhavam	7	15	nature
bhavan	1	8	respected you
bhavana	2	66	meditation
bhavapyayau	11	2	origin birth and death
bhavisyatam	10	34	of future things to come
bhaya-abhaye	18	3	fear and fearlessness

Sanskrit Word	Ch.	Slok	Meaning
bhayam	10	4	fear
bhayanakani	11	27	terrible
bhayavahah	3	35	that which causes fear
bhedam	17	7	classification
bheryah	1	13	kettle drums used in the war
Bhima-abhi rakshitam	1	1	in the care of Bhima
Bhima-Arjuna samah	1	4	equals of Bhima and Arjuna
bhimakarma	1	15	of fearful deeds
bhinna	7	4	is divided
Bhisma	1	11	The chief warrior of the Kaurava army; the scion of the family; He is the eighth son of King Sanatanu
Bhisma-Drona pramukhatah	1	25	in front of Bhisma and Drona
bhita-bhithah	11	35	fits of fear
bhitam	11	5	frightened one
bhoga-aisvarya gatim	2	43	attainment of enjoyment and prosperity
bhoga-aisvarya-prasaktanam	2	44	of those who are addicted to enjoyment and wealth
bhogaih	1	32	of enjoyments
bhogan	2	5	enjoyments
bhogi	16	14	one who enjoys
bhojanam	17	1	food
bhoksyase	2	37	you will enjoy
bhokta	9	24	one who enjoys

Sanskrit Word	Ch.	Slok	Meaning
bhoktaram	5	29	one who enjoys the fruits
bhoktrutve	13	2	enjoyment of happiness
bhoktum	2	5	to live and enjoy
bhraamayan	18	61	rotating
bhramati	1	3	whirls
Bhrguh	10	25	name of a sage
bhruvoh	5	27	of the eye-brows
bhumih	7	4	earth
bhungte	3	12	enjoys
bhunjanam	15	1	enjoying
bhutabhartr	13	16	supporter of beings
bhutadim	9	13	origin of all objects
bhuta-ganan	17	4	the hordes of spirits
bhuta-gramam	9	8	the five elements of creation-earth, water, fire, air and space
bhuta-maheswaram	9	11	the Lord of all beings
bhutanam	4	6	of beings
bhutani	2	28	all beings
bhuta-prakrti-moksam	13	34	liberation of beings from Prakrti
bhuta-prthak bhavam	13	3	diversity of living things
bhuta-sargau	16	6	creation of beings
bhutasthah	9	5	contained in the beings
bhut-bhrt	9	5	supporter of beings
bhutejyah	9	25	worshippers of elemental forces-like earth etc;

Sanskrit Word	Ch.	Slok	Meaning
bhutesa	10	15	the Lord of beings
bhutesu	7	11	among beings
bhutih	18	78	prosperity
bhuvi	18	69	in the world
bhuyah	2	2	again and again; more earnestly
bibharti	15	17	supports
bijam	7	1	seed
bija-pradah	14	4	who plants the seed
boddhavyam	4	17	to be known
bodhayantah	10	9	enlightening
brahma samsparsam	6	28	contact with Brahman
brahma-agnau	4	24	in the fire of Brahman
brahma-bhu tam	6	27	who has identified himself with Brahman
brahmacharyam	8	11	the disciplined life according to the scriptures, when the student studies at the master
Brahmakarma	18	42	here the word brahma is indicative of the person of knowledge and knowledge-profession; duties of Brahmanas
Brahma-karma samadhina	4	24	the yogic practice by which the supreme is realized
Brahman	3	15	The supreme force of creation; the unmanifest force
brahmana	4	24	by Brahman

Sanskrit Word	Ch.	Slok	Meaning
brahmana ksatriya-visam	18	41	The three social categories-knowledge worker; the warrior and the traders and service providers - the Brahmanas, the Ksatriyas and the Vaisyas
brahma-nirvaanam	2	72	identification with Brahman
brahma-sutra	13	4	Brahma-sutra is a vedanta
padaih			work; the formulae in this work and sentences of this work which lead to the knowledge of the Brahman
brahma-vadinam	17	24	of those who interpret the Vedas
brahma-vidah	8	24	knowers of Brahman
brahmi	2	72	of Brahman
brahmodbhavan	3	15	with Brahma as its source
bratrn	1	26	brothers
bravimi	1	7	I speak
bravisi	10	13	you speak
Brhaspatim	10	24	Brahaspati; Teacher of gods
Brhat-Sama	10	35	the foremost of the Sama hymns
bruhi	2	7	tell
buddhau	2	45	sheltering in the wisdom
buddhi-bhedam	3	26	doubt in understanding, confusion, second thought
buddhi-grahyam	6	21	can be grasped by intellect
buddhim	3	2	intellect
buddhiman	4	18	man of wisdom

Sanskrit Word	Ch.	Slok	Meaning
buddhi-matam	7	1	of the wise people
buddhi-nashah	2	63	loss of wisdom
buddhi-yogam	10	1	possession of wisdom
buddhi-yogat	2	49	from the yoga of wisdom
buddhi-yukta	2	5	possessed of wisdom
buddhva	3	43	after understanding
budhah	5	22	the wise one
cchandasam	10	35	of the metres
cchandobhih	13	4	vedic texts
cchetta	6	39	the dispeller
cchinna-abhram	6	38	scattered cloud
cchinnasamsaya	18	2	free from doubts
ccinna-dvaidha	5	25	whose doubts have been dispelled
chaila-ajina kusauttaram	6	11	cloth, deer skin and kusa grass placed to fom one seat.These are offered to the respected guests as a mark of holy welcome
chakra-hastam	11	46	with disc in hand, Krishna
chakram	3	16	wheel, disc, weapon of that shape
chakrinam	11	17	holding a disc, a name for Krishna who used the disc weapon as his favorite
chaksuh	5	27	eyes
chamum	1	3	army
chanchalam	6	26	restless

Sanskrit Word	Ch.	Slok	Meaning
chanchalatvat	6	33	owing to mental restlessness
chandramasam	8	25	lunar light
Chandramasi	15	12	in the moon
chapam	1	47	bow
chara-acharam	10	39	moving and non-me ring
chara-acharasya	11	43	moving and non-moving
charam	13	15	moving
charanti	8	11	practise
charatam	2	67	the wandering
charati	2	71	moves about
chaturbhujena	11	46	with four arms
chaturvidam	15	4	of four kinds
chaturvidhah	7	16	four classes
chatvarah	10	6	the four
Chekitanah	1	5	a renowned warrior in the army of the Pandavas
cheshtate	3	33	behaves
chet	2	33	if
chetana	10	22	intelligence
chetasa	8	8	mentally
chikrisuh	3	25	being desirous
chintayet	6	25	let him think
chintyantah	9	22	becoming meditative
chitrarathah	10	26	Chief of the Gandharvas
chittam	6	18	the mind
churnitaih	11	27	crushed

Sanskrit Word	Ch.	Slok	Meaning
chyavanti	9	24	they fail
dadami	10	1	I give
dadasi	9	27	you give
dahati	2	23	burns
daityanam	10	3	among the demons
daivah	16	6	divine
daivam	4	25	for the gods, related to gods
daivim	9	13	divine
daksah	12	6	who is clever
daksinayanam	8	25	southwardly movement of the sun with reference to the earth as the center of reference
daksyam	18	43	promptness
damah	10	4	self-control
dambha ahankara samyuktah	17	5	addicted to ostentation and pride
dambhah	16	4	ostentation
dambha-mana mada-anvitah	16	1	filled with vanity, conceit and arrogance
dambhartham	17	12	for ostentation
dambhena	16	17	with ostentation
danakriyah	17	25	charitable acts
danam	10	5	charity
danavah	10	14	demons
dandah	10	38	the rod
darpah	26	4	pride of wealth

Sanskrit Word	Ch.	Slok	Meaning
darpam	16	18	conceit
darsana kanksinah	11	52	eager to see
darsaya	11	4	show
dars'ayamasa	11	9	showed
dars'itam	11	47	has been shown
dasanantaresu	11	27	between the teeth
dasyante	3	12	will give
datavyam	17	2	ought to be given
dattam	17	28	offered in charity
daya	16	2	kindness
deha-bhrt	14	14	an embodied one
dehabhrta	18	11	for one who maintains a body
dehah	2	18	bodies
deham	4	9	body
dehantarapraptih	2	13	getting another body
dehasamud bhavan	14	2	which are having for their source the body-bodily born
dehavadbhih	12	5	by the embodied ones
dehi	2	22	the embodied being
dese	6	11	place
Deva	11	15	Gods, living at the heaven
devaanaam	10	2	of the gods
Devadattam	1	15	the name of the conch used by Arjuna. It was called Devadatta or God-given because it was gifted to him by Indra

Sanskrit Word	Ch.	Slok	Meaning
Devadeva	10	15	O, God of gods
Devadevasya	11	13	of the God of gods
devatah	4	12	the gods
dhanam	16	13	wealth
dhana-mana mada-anvitah	16	17	full of pride and arrogance of wealth
Dhananjaya	2	47	A name of Arjuna. It means one who has conquered wealth. Arjuna is so called because he acquired much wealth-human, divine, material and spiritual under the guidance of lord Krishna
dhanuh	1	2	bow
dhanurdharah	18	78	the wielder of the bow
dharayami	15	13	I support
dharayate	18	33	one controls
dharma atma	9	31	noble soul
dharma aviruddah	7	11	not opposed to righteousness
dharma sammudha-chetah	2	7	mind confused by incorrect understanding of the rules regarding the duty to be performed according to dharma
dharma-kama-arthan	18	34	righteousness, lust and wealth
Dharmakshetre	1	1	in the holy field of dharma

Sanskrit Word	Ch.	Slok	Meaning
dharmam	18	31	righteousness. Code of conduct governing the rights and responsibilities of individuals in society : it stands for that collective Indian conception of the religious, social and moral rule of conduct, the law of self-discipline and endeavor dharmic
dharmasya	2	3	of dharma
dharme	1	4	in righteousness
dharmyam	2	33	conducive to righteousness
dharmyamrtam	12	2	eternal wisdom
dharmyat	2	31	than righteous
Dhartarastrasya	1	23	of the sons of Dhrtarastra- the king of the Hastina town
dharyate	7	5	is supposed
dhata	9	17	dispenser
dhataram	8	9	the ordainer
dhirah	2	13	a wise person
dhiram	2	15	the wise man
Dhrstaketuh	1	5	name of a king on the Pandava side. Brother-in-law of Nakula. He was the king of the Cedi tribe
Dhrtarastrah	1	1	Eldest son of Vichitravirya and Ambika. He married Gandhari. Dhrtarastra was blind. But he was the king of the Kurus. Duryodhana is his eldest son

Sanskrit Word	Ch.	Slok	Meaning
dhrtim	11	24	firmness
dhruva	18	78	unfailing
dhruvam	2	27	eternal
dhumah	8	25	smoke
dhyanena	13	24	through meditation
dhyayantah	12	6	by thinking
dipta-anala-arka dhyutim	11	17	having the brilliance of the fire and the sun
dipta-hutasa vaktram	11	19	with a mouth from which blazing fire is coming out
divya-aneka udhyataayu dham	11	1	holding many uplifted divine weapons
divya-gandha anu-lepanam	11	11	annointed with divine perfumes
divyam	4	9	divine
doshaih	1	43	by defects and imperfections
dosham	1	38	evil
doshavat	18	3	sinful
doshena	18	48	with sin
drastum	11	3	to see
Draupadeyah	1	6	sons of Draupadi. Draupadi was the wife of the Pandavas. She was the daughter of Draupada, king of Panchala. Despite her dark complexion, she had a divine beauty which attracted numerous princes to her. She was married to the five Pandavas

Sanskrit Word	Ch.	Slok	Meaning
Dronah	11	26	The commander-in-chief of the Kurus at the battle of Kurukshetra. He was the preceptor of Arjuna in military science
druda vratah	7	28	firm in their beliefs
drudam	6	34	firm
drudena	15	3	with strength
Drupadah	1	4	Drupada was the king of Panchala. he was the father in law of the Pandavas
drusta-purvam	11	47	seen before
drustavan	11	52	you have seen
drustim	16	9	view
drustva	1	2	by seeing
dukham	5	6	sorrow
durasadam	3	43	difficult to control
durgatim	6	4	sad end
durlabhataram	6	42	very difficult
durniriksyam	11	17	difficult to see
duskrtam	4	8	of the wicked ones
duskrtinah	7	15	evil doers
dusprapa	6	36	hard to achieve
duspurena	3	39	which is insatiable
dustasu	1	41	corrupted
dvandvah	10	33	a compound of two or more words

Sanskrit Word	Ch.	Slok	Meaning
dvandva-moha vinir-muktah	7	28	being liberated from the delusion of duality
dvandva-mohena	7	27	by the delusion of duality
dvandvatitah	4	22	having gone beyond the dualities
dvaram	16	21	door
dvau	15	16	two
dvesah	13	6	aversion
dvesti	2	57	hates
dvesyah	9	29	hateful
Dvijottama	1	7	O, best of the twice-born or the Brahmin. The second birth is into the world of knowledge and mysticism. The individual born as a child of nature grows up into his spiritual manhood and becomes a child of light by the process of refinement attained
dvisatah	16	19	hateful
dvi-vidha	3	3	two kinds of
dyava-prthivyoh	11	2	between heaven and earth
dyutam	10	36	gambling
edha-msi	4	37	wooden pieces
ekam	3	2	single
eka-ntam	6	16	at all
ekastham	11	7	concentrated at one place

Sanskrit Word	Ch.	Slok	Meaning
esyasi	8	7	you will come
esyati	18	68	he will come
etaih	1	43	from these
eti	4	9	attains
evam	1	24	thus
evam vidah	11	53	in this manner
evam-rupah	11	48	in this form
gaam	15	13	the earth
gadinam	11	17	holding a mace, a name of Vishnu
gajendranam	10	27	among the elephants
gamyate	5	5	is reached
gandhah	7	9	fragrance
garbham	14	3	seed which caused the birth of all things
gariyah	2	6	better
gariyan	11	43	greater than
gariyase	11	37	who is greater
gata-agatam	9	21	going and returning
gatah	8	15	who have attained
gata-rasam	17	1	he which has lost it's taste and essence
gata-sandehah	18	73	with doubts dispelled
gatasangasya	4	23	who has abandoned attachment
gatasun	2	11	the departed
gatavyathah	12	16	who is fearless

Sanskrit Word	Ch.	Slok	Meaning
gatih	4	17	the real nature
gatim	6	37	goal
gavi	5	18	onacow
gehe	6	41	in the house
ghatayati	2	21	cause to be killed
ghoram	11	49	terrible
ghosah	1	19	uproar
ghraanam	15	9	nose
giram	10	25	of words
gitam	13	4	sung about
glanih	4	7	decline
ghnatah	1	35	killed
Govinda	1	32	name of
grasishnu	13	16	one who devours
guhyam	11	1	secret
guhyanam	10	3	of secret things
guhyatamam	9	1	highest secret
guhyataram	18	63	more secret
gunapravrdhah	15	2	strengthened by gunas
gunatitah	14	25	gone beyond the gunas
guruh	11	43	teacher
guruna	6	22	by the master / by the great
hanih	2	68	eradication
hanisye	16	14	I shall kill
hanta	10	19	now
hantaram	2	19	the killer

Sanskrit Word	Ch.	Slok	Meaning
hanti	2	19	kill
hantum	1	35	to kill
hanyate	2	19	killed
hanyuh	1	46	kill
haranti	2	6	carry away
harati	2	67	carries away
Hareh	18	77	of Narayana
Harih	11	9	Narayana
harsa-amarsa-bhaya-udvegaih	12	15	from joy, impatience, fear and worry
harsam	1	12	joy
harsa-soka-anvitah	18	27	liable to joy and sorrow
hastat	1	29	from the hand
hastini	5	18	on an elephant
hatah	2	37	has been killed
hatam	2	9	the killed
hatan	11	34	killed
hatva	1	31	by killing
havih	4	24	oblation
hayaih	1	14	horses
hetavah	18	5	causes
hetuh	13	2	cause
hetumadbhih	13	4	by the rational
hetuna	9	1	for this reason
Himalayah	16	25	The great mountains-the abode of snow
himsam	18	25	harm

Sanskrit Word	Ch.	Slok	Meaning
himsatmakah	18	27	naturally cruel
hinasti	13	28	harm
hita-kamyaya	10	1	wishing your welfare
hitam	18	64	beneficial
hitva	2	33	abandoning
hrdayadaurbalyam	2	3	mean weakness of the heart
hrdayani	1	19	the hearts
hrd-dese	18	61	in the area of the heart
hrdhyah	17	8	agreeable
hrdi	8	12	in the heart
hrih	16	2	modesty
Hrsikesa	11	36	name of Krishna
hrsitah	11	45	delighted
hrstaroma	11	14	with hairs standing on end
hrsyami	18	16	I rejoice
hrsyati	12	17	rejoices
hrta-jnanah	7	2	deprived of their wisdom
hrtoh	1	35	for the sake of
hrtstham	4	42	in the heart
hryate	6	44	carried forward
hutam	18	64	offered in sacrifice
iccha	12	9	desire
iccha-dvesa samutthena	7	27	by what originates from likes and dislikes
icchantah	8	11	desiring to know

Sanskrit Word	Ch.	Slok	Meaning
icchasi	11	7	you would desire
icchati	7	21	desires
idam	1	1	this
idanim	11	51	now
idrk	11	49	so much
idrsam	2	32	like this
idyam	11	44	worthy of worship
ihante	16	12	they strive
ihate	7	22	indulges in
ijyate	17	11	performed
ijyaya	11	53	by sacrifices
iksate	6	29	sees
Iksvakave	4	1	to Iksvaku who was the first among the kings of the Solar dynasty
indriya-arthebhyah	2	58	from the objects of senses
indriya.gocharah	13	5	sense objects which can be felt and experienced
indriya-aramah	3	16	who is happy in enjoying the pleasures of the senses; not going beyond it
indriya-arthan	3	6	objects of senses
indriya-arthasu	5	9	among the objects of senses
indriya-karmani	4	27	activities of senses
ingate	6	19	flickers
isam	11	15	lord of creatures
istah	18	64	dear

Sanskrit Word	Ch.	Slok	Meaning
ista-ka-ma dhuk	3	1	giver of desired objects.The reference is to the mystic desire yielding cow at heaven
istam	18	12	the desirable
isubhih	2	4	with arrows
isvarabhavah	18	43	godliness
isvarah	4	6	God
itarah	3	21	another
jaagratah	7	6	of the world
Jagannivasa	11	25	0 Lord of Universe
jagat	7	5	world
jaghanya guna vrttasthah	14	18	those who are involved in low quality actions
jagratah	6	16	one who keeps awake too long
jagrati	2	69	keeps awake
jahi	3	43	defeat
Jahnavi	19	31	The Ganges. The Ganges is the 39th longest river of the world and the 15th longest in Asia with a length of 2506 kilometres.But, from the point of view of sacredness, it is a river without a rival
janah	3	21	person
janan	8	27	has known
janati	15	19	knows
jane	11	25	know

Sanskrit Word	Ch.	Slok	Meaning
janma-karma phala pradam	2	43	result in rebirth as the fruit of their actions of birth janma-mrtyu and misery
janma-mrtyu jara-vyadhi duhkha- dosa anu-darsanam	13	8	seeing the evil in birth, death, old age, diseases and sorrows
jantavah	5	15	the creatures
japa-yajnah	10	25	ritual of meditation
jara	2	13	old age
jatasya	2	27	of one who is born
jatu	2	12	at anytime
jaya-ajayau	2	38	victory and defeat
Jayadrata	11	34	king of Sindhu, a warrior of Kaurava side; he was killed by Arjuna
jayah	10	36	splendour
jayante	14	12	come into existence
jayeha	2	6	they should conquer
jayema	2	6	we should conquer
jetasi	11	34	you shall conquer
jhasanam	10	31	among the whales - that type of water form of life
jinanagnih	4	37	the fire of knowledge
jitah	5	19	has been conquered
jivabhutam	7	5	which appears in the shape of individual souls
jivaloke	15	7	in the world of the living
jivanam	7	9	life, water

Sanskrit Word	Ch.	Slok	Meaning
jivati	3	16	lives
jnana dipena	10	11	with the lamp of knowledge
jnana-chaksusa	15	1	those with eyes of wisdom
jnana-dipite	4	27	which has been enlightened by knowledge
jnanam	18	5	the knowledge
jnana-nirdhuta kalmasah	5	1	their dirt having been removed by knowledge
jnana-sangena	14	6	through attachment to knowledge
jnanasina	4	42	with the sword of knowledge
jnanavan	3	33	man of wisdom
jnana-vijnana nasanam	3	41	destroyer of knowledge and discrimination
jnana-vijnana trpta-atma	6	8	whose mind is pleased with knowledge and realization
jnana-yajnah	4	33	sacrifice in which knowledge is substituted for all the materials of the sacrifice; or the knowledge acquiring-distribution-preservation is considered equivalent of sacrifice
jnana-yoga vya-vasthitih	16	1	perseverence in knowledge-yoga
jnani	7	16	man of knowledge
jnaninah	3	39	of the wise
jnasyasi	7	1	will know
jnatavyam	7	2	to be known

Sanskrit Word	Ch.	Slok	Meaning
jnatum	11	54	to be known
jnatva	4	15	having known
jneyah	5	3	should be known
jneyam	1	39	to be known
josayet	3	26	he should make them work
juhvati	4	26	offer
jvalanam	11	29	fire
jyayah	3	8	superior
jyayasi	3	1	is superior
jyotih	8	24	light
kaalam	8	23	time
kadachit	2	2	at any time
kala-anala samnibhani	11	25	resembling the flames of dissolution
kalah	10	3	time
kalayatam	10	3	among calculators of time
kalevaram	8	5	body
kalpadau	9	7	at the start of a yuga cosmic time cycle
kalpa-ksaye	9	7	at the end of a cosmic time cycle
kalpate	2	15	becomes worthy
kalyana-krt	6	4	doing good
kam	2	21	whom

Sanskrit Word	Ch.	Slok	Meaning
kamah	2	62	Desire. Cupid; basic universal desire which prompts action and pleasures
Kamala-patraksa	11	2	o, you, having eyes like lotus petals. This is an attribute of lord Vishnu because his eyes are beautiful like a lotus and of the shape of the leaf of the lotus
kamalasana stham	11	15	seated on lotus
kamatmanah	2	43	with minds full of desire
kama-upabhoga paramah	16	11	absorbed in the enjoyment of objects
kamepsuna	18	24	by one desiring results
Kandarpah	10	28	God of love, cupid
kapidhvajah	1	2	Arjuna, so-called because his flag had the emblem of Hanuman the great monkey god
Kapilah	10	26	the sage Kapila who is the founder of the samkhya system of philosophy
karanam	18	14	organs of actions
karanani	18	13	causes
karma	2	49	Action. An analysis of karma is given in Gita - verses chapter 3- (27-29); chap 4-(16-18); (6-14)
karma anubandhini	15	2	followed by action
karma bandhanah	3	9	becomes action-bound

Sanskrit Word	Ch.	Slok	Meaning
karma bandhanaih	9	28	from bondages of actions
karma phala asangam	4	2	attachment to the fruit of action
karma phalam	5	12	fruits of action
karma samudbhavah	3	14	born of action
karma-bandham	2	39	the bond of action
karma-chodana	18	18	incentive for action
karma-indriyani	3	6	organs of action
karmaja	4	12	from action
karmajam	2	51	caused by actions
karmajan	4	32	arising from action
karmanah	3	2	to action
karmanam	3	4	from actions
karmani	2	47	duty
karma-phala prepsuh	2	47	who desires the results of actions
karma-phala samyogam	5	14	association with the results of actions
karma-phala tyagai	12	12	renunciation of the fruits of action
karma-phalahetuh	2	47	fruits of action as the motive
karma-sangrahah	18	18	understanding of actions
karma-sanjnitah	8	3	meaning of action
karma-sanyasam	5	2	over renunciation of action
karmayogam	3	7	karma yoga- Ref. Gita (2-38,47,48,51)

Sanskrit Word	Ch.	Slok	Meaning
Karna	1	8	One of the chief warriors of Kaurava army; the friend of Duryodhana; by relation he was the eldest of the Pandava brothers; He was well known for his charity and generosity
karomi	5	8	I do
karoti	4	2	act
karsati	15	7	draws to itself
kartaram	4	13	agent
kartrtvam	5	14	agency
kartum	1	45	to do
karunah	12	13	one who is kind to all creatures
karya-akarye	18	3	duty and what is not duty
karyam	3	17	work to be done
karyate	3	5	to work
karye	18	22	form
kas'chit	2	17	perhaps
Kasirajah	1	5	King of Kasi - a warrior
kasmalam	2	2	dejection
kasmat	11	37	'why
kas'yah	1	17	Kasya, king of Kasi
katarat	2	6	which
kathanyatah	10	9	when he was speaking
kathaya	10	18	describe to me
katva-amla lavan atyusnatiksna ruksa-vidahinah	17	9	the tastes of bitter, sour, salty, very hot, pungent, dry and irritating

Sanskrit Word	Ch.	Slok	Meaning
kaumaram	2	18	boyhood
Kaunteya	2	14	o, son of Kunti; name of Arjuna
kausalam	2	5	cleverness
kavayah	4	16	the wise ones
kavim	8	9	the omniscient
kavinam	10	37	of the omniscient
kayam	11	4	body
Kesava	1	3	Name of Krishna
Kesavasya	11	35	of Kesava
kham	7	4	space
kilbisam	4	21	sin
kimacharah	14	21	of what conduct
kimchit	4	2	anything
kireetee	11	35	the crowned one; Arjuna
kiritinam	11	17	wearing a diadem
kirtayantah	9	14	extolling
kirtim	2	33	reputation
klaibhyam	2	3	cowardice
kledayanti	2	23	to make wet
Klesah	1	25	the struggle
kratuh	9	16	a sacrifice
kripaya	1	27	with pity
kriyate	17	18	undertaken
krodhah	2	62	anger
Krpah	1	8	brother-in-law of Drona

Sanskrit Word	Ch.	Slok	Meaning
Krsna	1	28	Krishna is the eighth avatar of Vishnu, the son of Vasudeva, brother of Kunti. Krishna is the most celebrated hero of Indian mythology and the most popular of all deities. Krishna is a divinity of remarkable psychologic
Krsnah	8	25	the dark fortnight
krupanah	2	49	to be pitied
kruta-anjalih	11	14	with folded hands
kruta-krutyah	15	2	duties done
krutam	4	15	done
kruta-nischayah	2	37	with firmness
krutena	3	18	with action
krutsna-karma-krt	4	18	doer of all actions
krutsnam	1	4	whole
krutsnasya	7	6	of the whole
krutsnavat	18	22	as if it were all
krutsna-vit	3	19	one who knows the All
krutva	2	38	having acted
ksahmi	12	13	who is forgiving
ksanam	3	5	moment
ksatra-karma	18	43	duties of Ksatriyas
kshama	10	4	forgiveness
kshantih	13	7	forgiveness
ksharam	15	18	the perishable

Sanskrit Word	Ch.	Slok	Meaning
kshayam	18	25	destruction, loss
kshemataram	1	46	better option and safer
kshetram	13	1	field
kshetri	13	33	knower of the field
kshina-kalmasah	5	25	whose sins have been destroyed
kshine	9	21	on the exhaustion
kshipami	16	19	I throw
kshudram	2	3	mean
ksipram	4	12	quickly
kuladharmah	1	4	family rituals
kulaghnanam	1	42	of those who have destroy the family
kulaks aye	1	4	in the process of the destruction of a family
kulaksayakrtam	1	38	the defects in the act of the destruction of a family
kulam	1	4	family
kulastriyah	1	41	women of the family
kulasya	1	42	of the family
Kuntibhojah	1	5	the name of a warrior
Kuntiputrah	1	16	Yudhishtira, son of Kunti
Kuru	2	48	undertake

Sanskrit Word	Ch.	Slok	Meaning
Kurukshetra	1	1	In Kurukshetra. Name of the place where the Mahabharata war was fought. The discourse between Krishna and Arjuna was held here before the war began. Kurukshetra has been described in the Mahabharata as bounded by the river Sarasvati on
Kuruvrddhah	1	12	eldest members of the Kuru family
kuryat	3	2	should do
kutah	2	2	how
kuurmah	2	58	tortoise
labdha	18	73	has been regained
labdham	16	13	has been gained
labdhva	4	39	obtaining
labha-alabhau	2	38	gain and loss
labham	6	22	gain
labhante	2	32	attain
labhasva	11	33	you gain
labhate	4	39	attains
labhe	11	25	find
labhet	18	8	acquire
labhyah	8	22	reached
laghavam	2	35	fall into disgrace
lelihyase	11	3	you lick your lips

Sanskrit Word	Ch.	Slok	Meaning
limpanti	4	14	taint
lingaih	14	21	signs
lipyate	5	7	tainted
lobhah	14	12	greed
lobhopahata chetasah	1	36	minds deluded by greed
loka maheswaram	10	3	great Lord of the worlds
lokah	3	9	man
loka-ksya-krt	11	32	destroying the world
lokam	9	33	world
loka-sangraham	3	2	guidance of mankind
lokasya	5	24	of all beings
lokat	12	15	by the world
loka-trayam	11	2	three worlds namely the Earth, Intermediate Space and Heaven
luptapindodaka kriyah	1	42	deprived of the offering of rice- balls and water to the manes
ma	2	3	do not
maardavam	16	2	gentleness
Maarga-shirsah	10	35	The lunar season relating to December-January
mad - yaaji	9	34	sacrifice to me
mad-ashrayah	7	1	taking refuge in me
mad-vyapasrayah	18	56	one who takes refuge in me
madam	18	35	pride and arrogance

Sanskrit Word	Ch.	Slok	Meaning
mad-anugrahaya	11	1	for my blessings
mad-arpanam	9	27	your offer to me
mad-artham	12	1	for me
mad-bhaktah	9	34	devoted to me
mad-bhaktesu	18	68	to my devotees
mad-bhaktim	18	54	devotion to me
mad-bhavah	10	6	through their thoughts on me
mad-bhavam	4	1	my state
mad-bhavhya	13	18	for my state
mad-gata-pranah	10	9	whose lives are dedicated to me
mad-gatena	6	47	fixed on me
Madhava	1	37	One of the thousand names of Vishnu (Krishna)
Madhusudana	1	35	name of Krishna
madh-yajinah	9	25	those who worship me
madhyam	10	2	middle
mad-yogam	12	11	to the yoga for me
maha-baho	2	26	O, mighty armed one, name of Arjuna
mahabhutani	13	5	The great elements which constitute the universe, namely, the ether, air, fire, water and earth. They are present in the entire universe though not evenly distributed
mahad-brahma	14	3	the great Brahman
mahadh-yonih	14	4	great womb

Sanskrit Word	Ch.	Slok	Meaning
mahan	9	6	great
mahanubhavan	2	5	noble minded
maha-papma	3	37	great sinner
maharathah	1	4	great warriors
maharsayah	10	2	the great sages
maharsi-siddha sangah	11	21	groups of great sages
mahasankham	1	15	the great conch, named Paundra
mahashanah	3	37	all-consuming
mahatmanah	11	12	of the great soul
mahatmyam	11	2	glory
maheekrute	1	35	for the earth
mahesvasah	1	4	wielding great bows
maheswarah	13	22	the great God
mahiksitam	1	25	rulers of the earth
mahimanam	11	41	greatness
mahipate	1	2	O, king
maitrah	12	13	he who is friendly
makarah	10	31	shark
malena	3	38	by dirt
mamakah	1	1	my
mamakam	15	12	mine
mamikam	9	7	to mine
mamsyante	2	35	will think
mana apamanayoh	6	7	in honour and dishonour

Sanskrit Word	Ch.	Slok	Meaning
manah	1	3	mind
manah-pranen driya-kriyah	18	33	functions of the mind, life, forces and organs
manah-prasadah	17	16	tranquility of mind
manah-shasthani	15	7	which have the mind as their sixth sense
manasa	3	6	mentally
manasah	10	6	from mind
manasam	17	61	mental
Manavah	10	6	to Manu
manavah	3	31	men
Manave	4	1	to Manu
mandaan	3	29	of poor intellect
mani-ganah	7	7	pearls on string, necklace
manisinah	2	51	learned persons
manogatan	2	55	desires, which have entered the mind
manoratham	16	13	desired object
mantavyah	9	3	to be considered
mantra-hinam	17	13	where mantras are not recited
manusam	11	51	human
manuse-loke	16	2	in the human world
manusim	9	11	human
manusyaloke	15	2	into the world of men
manusyanam	1	44	among men
manusyesu	4	18	of men
manyate	2	19	thinks

Sanskrit Word	Ch.	Slok	Meaning
maranat	2	34	than death
Marichi	10	21	Marichi - name of the chief of Maruts
martya-lokam	9	21	human world
Marutah	11	6	a group of wind gods
masaanam	10	35	of the lunar based caluculation of the months
mata	3	1	thought
mata	9	17	mother
matah	6	32	is regarded
matam	3	31	teaching
mat-chittah	10	9	with minds fixed on me
matih	6	36	faith, mind
mat-paramh	12	2	who regards me (as the Supreme Goal)
mat-samstham	6	15	which abides in me
matsthani	9	4	abide in me
matulah	1	34	maternal uncles
matva	3	28	thinking
maunam	10	38	silence
mauni	12	19	one who is silent
mayaya	7	15	by maya
mayaya	7	14	Cosmic illusion
medhah	10	34	intelligence
medhavi	18	1	intelligent person
Meruh	10	23	Mountain of gods; golden mountain

Sanskrit Word	Ch.	Slok	Meaning
misram	18	12	the mixed
mithya	18	59	vain, false hood
mithya-acharah	3	6	a hypocrite
mitradrohe	1	38	cheating and treachery towards friends
modisye	16	15	I shall hopes
mogha- jnanah	9	12	of vain knowledge
mogha-karmanah	9	12	of vain actions
mogham	3	16	in vain
moha-jala samavrutah	16	16	trapped in the web of ilusion
moha-kalilam	2	52	confusion of delusion
moham	4	35	delusion
mohanam	14	8	delusive
mohayasi	3	2	you confuse me
moksa-kan- ksibhih	17	25	by persons desiring salvation
moksam	18	1	salvation
moksa- parayanah	5	28	fully desiring salvation
moks'aya	7	29	for freedom from old age and death-
moksayase	4	16	you will be liberated
moksayisyami	18	66	I shall liberate you
mrityum	13	25	death
mriyate	2	2	dies
mrtasya	2	27	of the dead
mrtyu-samsara vart-mani	9	3	along the path of the living mortals

Sanskrit Word	Ch.	Slok	Meaning
mrtyu-samsara-sagarat	12	7	from the sea of the mortal world of death
mruganam	10	3	among animals
mrugendra	10	3	lion
mrutam	2	29	dead
muchyante	3	13	become freed
muda-yonisu	14	16	in the wombs of the foolish
muhuh	18	76	moment
muhyati	2	13	is deluded
mukham	1	28	face, opening, mouth
mukhani	11	25	faces, moths , openings
mukhyam	10	24	the most important
mukta sangah	3	9	free from attachment
muktah	5	28	liberated
muktam	18	4	freed
muktasya	4	23	of the liberated person
muktva	8	5	by abandoning
mulani	15	2	roots
mumuksubhih	4	15	seekers of salvation
munayah	14	1	monks
munih	2	56	monk
murdhani	8	12	in the head
muuda-grahena	17	19	with a foolish purpose
na	1	32	not
nabhah	1	19	sky
nabhah-sprsam	11	24	reaching heaven

Sanskrit Word	Ch.	Slok	Meaning
naganam	10	29	among snakes or the elephants or the people of this class
naiskarmya siddhim	18	49	supreme state of freedom from duties
naiskarmyam	3	4	freedom from action
naiskritikah	18	28	cruel
naisthikim	5	12	arising from firmness
Nakulah	1	11	Nakula and Sahadeva were the twin brothers born to Madri, second wife of King Pandu
namaskuru	9	34	bow down
nama-yajnaih	16	17	type of meditation in which the name of the lord is repeated. Such repetition is also considered equivalent to the ritualistic sacrifice
nara-adhaman	16	19	lowest among men
Naradah	10	13	A divine sage-Devarishi. He was the son of Brahma and devotee of Vishnu. Narada was an expert in law and the author of the book, Naradiya Dharma-Sastra. A book explaining the true secret of devotion and how the devotee should behave

Sanskrit Word	Ch.	Slok	Meaning
narakasya	16	21	of hell. In Verse 21 of Chapter XVI Krishna says that lust, anger and greed constitute the triple gates of hell and therefore one should avoid these. Seven hells are listed in the texts. These are the places where the dead suffer punishment for their evil
narake	1	44	in hell
nara-loka virah	11	28	heroes of the world men
naranam	10	27	among men
narapungavah	1	5	the best among men
narinam	10	34	of the woman
nasa-abhyantara charinau	5	27	that which goes through the nostrils
nasanam	16	21	destroyer
nasayami	10	11	I destroy
nastan	3	32	to have been ruined
nasthah	4	2	is lost
nas'yati	6	38	is ruined
nava-dvare	5	13	This word refers to the human body which has nine entry-exit points for the life to enter into this mortal coil
navani	2	22	new ones
nibaddah	18	6	being strongly body
nibadhnati	14	7	binds
nibandhaya	4	41	for binding purpose only

Sanskrit Word	Ch.	Slok	Meaning
nibodha	1	7	learn
nidhanam	3	35	death
nidra-alasya pramada uttham	18	39	originating from sleep, lethargy and indifference
nigacchati	9	31	he attains
nigrahah	3	33	control
nigrhitani	2	68	are withdrawn
nigrhnami	9	19	I withdraw
nihatah	11	33	have been surely killed
nihatya	1	36	by killing
nihspruhah	2	71	free from covetousness
nimisan	5	9	shutting the eyes
nimitta-matram	11	33	merely a tool
nimittani	1	3	omens
nindantah	2	36	while deprecating
nirasih	3	3	free from hope
nirgunam	13	14	without quality
nirgunatvat	13	31	devoid of qualities
nirikshe	1	22	observe
niruddam	6	2	controlled
nirvairah	11	55	who is free from enmity
nirvedam	2	52	dispassion
nirvikarah	18	26	un perturbed
nis'chala	2	53	unshakable
nischarati	6	26	wanders
nis'chayam	18	4	certainly

Sanskrit Word	Ch.	Slok	Meaning
nischayena	6	23	with firmness
nis'chitam	2	7	firm
nischitya	3	2	for certain
nishs'reyasa karau	5	2	lead to salvation
nistraigunyah	2	45	free from the three qualities of Sattva, Rajas and Tamas
nitih	10	38	right policy
nityah	2	2	eternal
nityajatam	2	26	constantly born
nityam	2	2	eternal
nitya-sanyasi	5	3	a man of constant renunciation
nitya-truptah	4	2	constant concentration
nitya-vairina	3	39	constant enemy
nityayuktah	7	17	constant firmness
nitya-yuktasya	8	14	of constant concentration
nivaasah	9	18	abode
nivartante	8	21	they return
nivartanti	15	4	return
nivartitum	1	39	to turn away
nivasisyasi	12	8	you will dwell
nivata-sthah	6	19	located in a place away from wind
nivesaya	12	8	rest
nivruttani	14	22	when they disappear
nivruttim	16	7	withdrawal
niyaman	7	2	methods

Sanskrit Word	Ch.	Slok	Meaning
niyatah	7	2	regulated
niyataharah	4	3	having their food controlled
niyatam	1	44	daily
niyata-manasah	6	15	of controlled mind
niyatasya	18	7	of the daily obligatory duties
niyatatmabhih	8	2	by controlled minds
no	17	28	no
nru loke	11	48	in the world of man
nrushu	7	8	in men
nu	1	35	then
nyayyam	18	15	righteous
ojasa	15	13	through power
paapah	3	13	impure persons
paapa-krit-tamah	4	36	the worse sinner
paapat	1	39	from sin
paapa-yonayah	9	32	born of sin
paapena	5	1	by sin
paatakam	1	38	sin
pachami	15	14	digest
pachanti	3	13	cook
paksinam	10	3	among birds
panava-anaka gomukhah	1	13	war drums and instruments tabors, drums and horns
panca	13	5	five

Sanskrit Word	Ch.	Slok	Meaning
Panchajanyam	1	15	Name of Krishna's conch. It is made from the bones of a demon, named Panchajana, who lived under the sea and was killed by Krishna. The sound of this conch created terror in the minds of enemies
Pandavah	1	1	Pandavas were the sons of Pandu who was the brother of Dhritarastra and king of Hastinapura. The five sons of Pandu are Yudhisthira, Bhima, Arjuna, Nakula and Sahadeva
panditah	2	11	learned ones
panditam	4	19	learned
Panduputranam	1	3	of the sons of Pandu
papebhyah	4	36	than sinners
papesu	6	9	among sinners
papmanam	3	4	sinful
para-dharmah	3	35	another's dharma
para-dharmat	3	35	than another's dharma
parama-atma	6	7	supreme self
paramah	6	32	the best
Parama-isvara	11	3	0 Supreme Lord
paramam	8	3	highest
paramam	8	13	supreme
parampara- praptam	4	2	received through a regular succession of tradition

Sanskrit Word	Ch.	Slok	Meaning
Parantapa	2	3	scorcher of foes-a name of Arjuna
parastat	8	9	beyond
paratah	3	42	superior
parataram	7	7	higher
parisamapyate	4	33	get merged
parisusyati	1	28	dries up
parjanyah	3	14	rainfall
parjanyat	3	14	from rainfall
parnani	15	1	leaves
Partha	1	25	another name of Arjuna
parusyam	16	4	haughtiness
paryaptam	1	1	limited
paryavatisthate	2	65	becomes well established
paryupasate	4	25	undertake
paryusitam	17	1	stale
pasya	1	3	behold
pasyami	1	31	I see
pasyan	5	8	while seeing
pasyanti	1	38	they see
pasyatah	2	69	to those who see
pasyati	2	29	sees
pas'yet	4	18	finds
patangah	11	29	moths
patanti	1	42	fall
patram	9	26	a leaf

Sanskrit Word	Ch.	Slok	Meaning
paurusam	7	8	manliness and courage
paurva-dehikam	6	43	related to the body of the previous birth
pautran	1	26	grandsons
pavakah	2	2	fire
pavanani	18	5	the purifiers
pavatam	10	31	among the purifiers
pavitram	4	38	purifying
phala-akanksi	18	34	desiring their results
phala-hetavah	2	49	who are eager for results
phalam	2	51	result
phalani	18	6	results
pidaya	17	19	causing pain
pita	9	17	father
pitamah	1	12	grandfather
pitarah	1	33	forefathers
pitruunam	10	29	among the manes
pitru-vratah	9	25	followers of the manes
praapnuyat	18	71	shall attain
prabha	7	8	effulgence
prabhaseta	2	54	speak
prabhavam	10	2	source of emergence
prabhavisnu	3	16	the originator
prabhuh	5	14	the self
pradhanyatah	10	19	according to their significance
pradiptam	11	29	shining

Sanskrit Word	Ch.	Slok	Meaning
pradistam	8	28	ordained by the scripture
pradusyanti	1	41	become impure
pradvisanti	16	18	hate each other
praha	4	1	told; instructed
praharsyet	5	2	he should be happy
prahasan	2	1	with a smile
Prahlada	10	3	son of the demon king Hiranyakasipu
prahrsyati	11	36	will become happy
prajah	3	1	the beings
prajahati	2	55	when one completely gives up, renounces
prajanah	10	28	the projenitor
prajanati	18	31	when one realises
prajapatih	3	1	Father of mankind
prajna	2	57	wisdom
prajnam	2	67	final wisdom arising from the knowledge of distinction between self and non-self
prajnavadan	2	11	speech wich imitates the speech of the learned persons
prajuyyate	17	26	is used
prak	5	23	before
praka-sah	7	25	shining
prakasakam	14	6	an illuminator
prakasam	14	22	light
prakasayati	5	16	reveals

Sanskrit Word	Ch.	Slok	Meaning
prakirtya	11	36	after praising
prakritah	18	28	uncivilized
prakrti sambhavan	13	19	born out of natural temparament and disposition
prakrtih	7	4	nature; divine power, identified with sakti and maya the source of creation; the form a, expression and power of the Lord
prakrti-stani	15	7	which is seated in nature
prakrtisthah	13	21	enshrined in nature
prakrutijan	13	21	born of nature
pralapan	5	9	speaking
pralayam	14	14	final cosmic dissolution
pralayantam	16	11	that which survives up to the end of the dissolution
pralaye	14	2	during dissolution
pralinah	14	15	when one dies
praliyate	8	19	disappears
pramada-alasya nidrabhih	14	8	through carelessness, laziness and sleep
pramadah	14	13	carelessness
pramadat	11	41	through carelessness
pramanam	3	21	authority
pramathi	6	34	which causes turbulence
pramuchyate	5	3	is liberated
pramukhe	2	6	in front

Sanskrit Word	Ch.	Slok	Meaning
prana-apana sama-yuktah	15	14	in conjunction with prana and apana forces of vital air
prana-apana-gati	4	29	movements of outgoing and inhaling breaths
pranakarmani	4	27	the life function of the vital organs
pranam	4	29	breath, life force
pranamya	11	14	after bowing down
pranastah	18	72	self-destroyed
pranasyati	2	63	he is doomed
pranavah	7	8	sacred letter Om
pranayama parayanah	4	29	Yogic way to control the life force-regularly practising control of the vital forces
pranayena	11	41	out of love rising out of intimacy
pranesu	4	3	in the vital forces
pranidhaya	11	34	After prostrating - before the elders/gods/learned persons
praninam	15	14	of creatures
pranipatena	4	14	by bodily salutation in which the student falls falt on the ground before the master and seeks his blessings
pranjalayah	11	21	saluting with respect with the hands folded and palms together
prapadyate	7	19	attains
prapadye	15	4	I take refuge in you

Sanskrit Word	Ch.	Slok	Meaning
prapannam	2	7	those who have taken refuge
prapasya	11	49	see well
prapasyadbhi	1	39	seeing very well with clear mind and sight
prapasyami	2	8	I see clearly
pra-pitamahah	11	39	the great grandfather
praptah	18	5	achieved
prapya	2	57	after reaching
prarabhate	18	15	performs
prarthayante	9	2	offering prayers
prasabham	2	6	without proper care
prasadam	2	64	tranquillity
prasadaye	11	44	I try to propitiate
prasaktah	16	16	absorbed
prasangena	18	34	as the situation arises
prasanna-cetasah	2	65	of one with peace of mind
prasannena	11	47	by the grace of
prasanta manasam	6	27	whose mind has become completely calm
prasantasya	6	7	of one who is of cool mind
prasantatma	6	14	with a peaceful mind
prasaste	17	26	auspicious
prasavisyadhvam	3	1	you support each other
praseeda	16	25	be pleased
prasiddhyet	3	8	will be possible
prasrtah	15	2	extending
prasruta	15	2	has occurred, spread all over

Sanskrit Word	Ch.	Slok	Meaning
pratapanti	11	3	burning due to heat and scorching
pratapavan	1	12	one who has courage
prathitah	15	18	well known
prati	2	43	about; this is an indeclinable form of word
pratijane	18	65	I understand like this
pratijanihi	9	31	You understand like this.
pratipadyate	14	14	he obtains
pratistha	4	27	that abode/support in which something dwells
pratisthapya	6	11	having established
pratisthitam	3	15	established
pratiyotsyami	2	4	I fight against the warriors of the enemy camp
pratyaksa avagamam	9	2	directly realisable and experiencable
pratyanikesu	11	32	in the armies of the enemies
pratyavayah	2	4	trouble, disturbance, blocking, obstructing
pratyupakara artham	17	21	expecting reciprocity
pravadanti	2	42	they speak
pravadatam	10	32	of those who debate
pravartate	5	14	engage in actions
pravartitam	3	16	set in motion
pravestum	11	54	to be entered into
pravibhaktam	11	13	differentiated

Sanskrit Word	Ch.	Slok	Meaning
pravibhaktani	18	41	have been grouped
pravillyate	4	23	is destroyed
pravisanti	2	7	enter
pravksayami	4	16	I shall tell
pravrddah	11	32	grown, improved
pravrittih	14	12	movement
pravruttah	11	32	engaged
pravruttim	11	31	actions
pravyathita antara-atma	11	24	becoming agitated in my mind
pravyathitam	11	2	struck with great fear and disturbed
prayana-kale	7	3	at the last moment of death
prayata	8	23	they have also gone by the same path
prayat-atmanah	9	26	a person who has made efforts to achieve
prayati	8	5	leaves
prayatnat	6	45	by effort
prayuktah	3	36	forced to do, empowered, motivated
preeta-manah	11	49	pleased in mind
preeti-purvakam	10	1	with love
preeyamanaya	10	1	who is happy
pretan	17	4	ghosts of deceased persons
pretya	17	28	after death
pritih	1	36	pleasure, affection

Sanskrit Word	Ch.	Slok	Meaning
pritivee pate	1	18	O king
priyachikirsavah	1	23	those who are desirous of pleasing
priyah	7	17	dear
priyahitam	17	15	dear and beneficial
priya-krttamah	18	69	one who does only those deeds which are liked by; the best amongst such persons
priyam	5	2	what is pleasing
priyatarah	18	69	dearer
prochyamanam	18	29	while it is being stated
prochyate	18	19	are stated
prokta	3	3	were spoken of
proktah	4	3	has been taught
proktam	8	1	is spoken of
proktani	18	13	which have been spoken of
proktavan	4	1	proclaimed
protam	7	7	is strung
prthagdvidhan	18	21	of different kinds
prthak	1	18	as seaperated
prthaktvena	9	15	in distinct and seperate forms
prthivyam	7	9	in this earth
prthvim	1	19	earth
prucchami	2	7	I seek and request you
prusthatah	11	4	behind
pujarhau	2	4	worthy of respect
Pujyah	11	43	worthy of honour

Sanskrit Word	Ch.	Slok	Meaning
puman	2	71	man
pumsah	2	62	of the individual
punah	4	9	again
punyah	7	9	sacred
punyakarmanam	7	28	of those who do noble deeds
punyakrtam	6	41	those who are righteous
punyam	9	2	virtuous and meritorious deeds and the fruit of it
punya-phalam	8	28	fruits of noble deeds
pura	3	3	in ancient times
puranah	2	2	timeless and belonging to the past; very old
puranam	8	9	the ancient
purani	15	4	of the past; ancient
purastat	11	4	in the front
puratanah	4	3	belonging to the past
purodhasam	10	24	among priests
Purujit	1	5	Purujit - the name of a warrior; (see Kuntibhoja)
purusah	2	21	man; a generic name for all human beings
Purusarsabha	2	15	A title; like a bull among men; name of Arjuna
purusasya	2	6	of a person
Purusa-vyaaghra	18	4	An adjective- like a tiger among men, name of Arjuna
Purusottama	8	1	The supreme being; best among men

Sanskrit Word	Ch.	Slok	Meaning
purva-abhyasena	6	44	by past practice
purvaih	4	15	by the seers of the yore
purvataram	4	15	the previous one
puskalabhih	11	21	detailed, plentily, without limit
pusnami	15	13	I make them grow and nourish
puspam	9	26	flower
puspitam	2	42	This is a poetic usage. It means that which has come out like the flower from the tree; the best output
putah	4	1	purified
puta-papah	9	2	who are freed from sin due to the grace of the lord; or their meritorious deeds
puti	17	1	putrid
putra-dara gruhadisu	13	9	regarding the issues like sons and wife and home
putrasya	11	44	of the son
raga-dvesa viyuktaih	2	64	which are free from attraction and aversion
raga-dvesau	3	34	attraction and aversion
ragatmakam	14	7	of passionate nature
ragi	18	27	who is attached
rahasi	6	1	in a solitary place
rahasyam	4	3	secret
raja	1	2	king
raja-guhyam	9	2	royal wisdom

Sanskrit Word	Ch.	Slok	Meaning
rajan	11	9	O king
rajarsayah	4	2	royal sages; men who were kings and sages at the same time
Rajasah	14	16	of the temperament of the quality called rajas
rajasam	17	12	done through rajas
rajasasya	17	9	having rajas
raja-vidhya	9	2	sovereign knowledge
rajoguna samudhbhavah	3	37	originating from the quality of rajas
rajyam	8	17	kingdom
rajyasukhalobhena	1	45	for the joys of a kingdom
rajyena	1	32	for a kingdom
raksamsi	11	36	Raksasas
raksasim	9	12	of demons
Ramah	10	31	Sri Rama - the chief character of the epic Ramayana. There are three personalities called Rama in indian mythology- One is Sri Rama, Second is Parashu Rama; the third is Balarama. The first two are the avatars of lord Vishnu; the third is the brother of Sri Krishna
ramanti	10	9	they enjoy
ramate	5	22	enjoys
ranaat	2	35	from battle
rasah	2	59	taste

Sanskrit Word	Ch.	Slok	Meaning
rasanam	15	9	tongue
rasatmakah	15	13	watery
rasavarjam	2	59	excepting the taste
rasyah	17	8	juicy
ratah	5	25	who are engaged
ratham	1	21	chariot
rathopasthe	1	47	near the chariot
rathottamam	1	24	splendid chariot
ratrih	8	25	night
ratrya-agame	8	18	when night comes
ravih	10	21	the Sun
ripuh	6	5	enemy
Rk	9	17	Rig Veda - one of the four vedas and the first amongst them
roma-harsanam	18	74	the experience which makes hair stand on end
rshayah	5	25	the sages
rsheen	11	15	sages
rshibhih	13	4	by the sages
rtam	10	14	cosmic law of righteousness
rte	11	32	without
rtunam	10	35	of the seasons
ruddhva	4	29	by stopping
rudhirapradigdhan	2	5	drenched in blood
Rudra-Adityah	11	22	Rudras and Adityas
Rudranam	10	23	among the Rudras

Sanskrit Word	Ch.	Slok	Meaning
rupam	11	3	form
sa	2	69	that
sa-adhi-bhuta-adhidaivam	7	3	as dwelling in the material and the divine planes
sa-adhiyajnam	7	3	as existing in relation to sacrifice
sabda-brahma	6	44	result of vedic rites
sabdadin	4	26	originating from sound
sabdah	1	13	sound
sacchabdah	17	26	the word "sat"
sachara-acharam	9	1	with the moving and non-moving thing
sachetah	11	51	calm in mind
sada	5	28	always
sad-asadh-yoni-janmasu	13	21	born in wombs good and bad
sad-bhave	17	26	goodness
sadharmyam	14	2	identify with nature
sadhu-bhave	17	26	in the sense of goodness
sadhunam	4	8	of the good people
sadhusu	6	9	regarding good people
sadhyah	11	22	a class of demi-gods
sadosam	18	48	faulty
sadrsam	3	33	comparable
sadrsi	11	12	similar
saduh	9	3	good

Sanskrit Word	Ch.	Slok	Meaning
sagadgadam	11	35	with faltering voice
sagarah	10	24	ocean
saha	1	2	along with
Sahadevah	1	16	the youngest of the Pandu princes
sahajam	18	48	to which one is born
sahankarena	18	24	by one who is egoistic
sahasa	1	13	suddenly
sahasra-baho	11	46	O, you with a thousand hands
sahasra-krtvah	11	3	a thousand times
sahasrasah	11	51	in thousands
sahasra-yuga-par-yantam	8	17	ends in a thousand yugas
sahasresu	7	13	among thousand
saha-yajnah	3	1	together with the sacrifices
sainyasya	1	7	of the army
sajiante	3	29	they become attached
sajiate	3	28	becomes attached
sakha	4	3	friend
sakhe	11	41	O, friend
sakhyuh	11	44	of a friend
saknomi	1	3	I can
saknosi	12	9	you can
saknoti	5	23	one who can
saksat	18	75	actually
saksi	9	18	witness
saktah	3	25	being confined

Sanskrit Word	Ch.	Slok	Meaning
saktam	18	22	confined
sakyah	6	36	possible
sakyam	11	4	possible
sakyase	11	8	you can
sama	9	17	Sama Veda
sama-buddha yah	12	4	being even attain
sama-buddhih	6	9	equal minded
samachara	3	9	you perform
samacharan	3	26	performing
sama-chittatvam	13	9	mental equanimity
sama-darsinah	5	18	look equally
samadhatum	12	9	to establish
samadhau	2	44	in the minds
samadhaya	17	11	conviction
samadhi-gacchati	3	4	does he attain
samadhi-sthasya	2	54	of a man of firm wisdom
sama-duhkha sukham	2	15	same attitude in sorrow and happiness
sama-duhkha-sukhah	12	13	one to whom sorrow and happiness are the same
samagatah	1	23	who have assembled
samagram	4	23	the whole
samah	6	3	inaction
samah	2	48	same
samah	6	41	years
samahartum	11	32	in destroying
samahitah	6	7	become manifest

Sanskrit Word	Ch.	Slok	Meaning
samaksam	11	42	in public
sama-losta-asama kanchanab	6	8	to whom a piece of earth, steel and gold are the same
samam	11	24	peace
samam	5	19	equality
samantatah	6	24	from every side
samapasthitam	1	28	arrayed
samapnosi	11	4	you pervade
samarambhah	4	19	actions
samarthyam	2	36	strength
samasaresu	16	19	in the worlds
samasatah	13	18	briefly
samasena	13	3	briefly
samasi-kasya	10	33	of the group of compound words
samata	10	5	equanimity
samatijayah	1	8	ever victorious
samatitani	7	26	the past beings
samatitya	14	26	having gone beyond
samatvam	2	48	equanimity in success and defeat
samavasthitam	13	28	present alike
sama-vedah	10	22	Sama veda
samavetah	1	1	they assembled
samavetan	1	25	assembled
sambandhinah	1	34	relatives
Sambhavah	14	3	birth

Sanskrit Word	Ch.	Slok	Meaning
sambhavami	4	6	I am born
sambhavanti	14	4	are born
sambhavitasya	2	34	to a worthy person
samdrsyante	11	27	are seen
samgrahena	8	11	briefly
samgramam	2	33	battle
samharate	2	58	fully withdrawn
samidhah	4	37	blazing
samiksya	1	27	having seen
samistabhya	3	43	fully establishing
Samjanayan	1	12	causing
samjnartham	1	7	for information
samkalpa-prabhavan	6	24	which arrive from thoughts
samkarah	1	42	confusion
samkarasya	3	29	intermingling
samkhye	1	47	in the battle
sammoham	7	27	deluded
sammohat	2	63	from delusion
samnam	10	35	of the Sama mantras
samniyamya	12	4	by completely controlling
sampad	16	5	wealth
sampadhyate	13	3	becomes identified
sampasyan	3	2	with a view to
samplutodake	2	46	when it is flooded
samprakirtitah	18	4	has been clearly explained

Sanskrit Word	Ch.	Slok	Meaning
sampravrttani	14	22	when they appear
sampreksya	6	13	looking
samrddham	11	33	prosperous
samrddha-vegah	11	29	with great haste
samsaya-atmanah	4	4	who has a doubting mind
samsayah	8	5	doubt
samsayam	4	42	doubt
samsayasya	6	39	of doubt
samsiddhau	6	43	for success
samsiddhim	3	2	complete success
samsita-vratah	4	28	in observing severe vows
samsmrtya	18	76	while remembering
samsparsajah	5	22	arising from contact with objects
samsritah	6	18	resorting to
samsuddha-kilbisah	6	45	becoming absolved from sin
samtarisyasi	4	36	you will cross over
samud ram	2	7	ocean
samuddharta	12	7	the deliverer
samupasrita	18	52	endowed with
samvadam	18	7	conversation
samvrttah	11	51	become
samyak	5	4	properly
samya-matam	10	29	among those who keep the law
samyami	2	69	the self-controlled man
samyamya	2	61	by controlling

Sanskrit Word	Ch.	Slok	Meaning
samyateindriyah	4	39	whose senses are controlled
samyati	2	22	goes
samye	5	19	on sameness
samyena	6	33	as sameness
sanaih	6	25	gradually
sanatanah	2	24	eternal
sanatanam	4	31	eternal
sangah	2	47	inclination
sangam	2	48	attachment
sanga-rahitim	18	23	without attachment
sangat	2	62	from attachment
sanga-varjitah	11	55	free from attachment
sanga-vivarjitah	12	18	free from attachment to everything
Sanjaya	1	1	Literally, one whose victory is complete
sanjayate	2	62	is born
sanjayati	14	9	leads
sankhah	1	13	conchs
sankhyaih	5	5	by the sankhyas
sankhyam	5	5	Literally, it means counting
sankhyanam	3	3	for men of renunciation
sankhya-yogau	5	4	of Sankhya Yoga
sankhye	2	39	in Sankhya
sankhyena	13	24	by the sankhyas
sanmasah	8	24	six months
san-nivistah	15	15	seated

Sanskrit Word	Ch.	Slok	Meaning
sannyasah	5	2	renunciation
sannyasam	5	1	renuniciation
sannyasanat	3	4	through renunciation
sannyasasya	18	1	about renunciation
sannyasa-yoga-yukta-atma	9	28	The soul endowed with the yoga of renunciation
sannyasena	18	49	through renunciation
sannyasi	6	1	a monk
sannyasinam	18	12	to those who resort to renunciation
sannyasya	3	3	by dedicating
sanrani	2	22	bodies
santah	3	13	by being
santustah	3	17	who is satisfied
sapatnan	11	34	enemies
sapta	10	6	seven
sarapam	2	49	refuge
sarasam	10	24	among large lakes
sargah	5	19	rebirth
sarganam	10	32	of creations
sarge	7	27	during creation
sarhyama-agnisu	4	26	in the fires of self-discipline
sarira vimokasnat	5	23	departing from the body
sariram	13	1	body
sariranah	2	18	embodied one
sarirastham	17	6	in the body

Sanskrit Word	Ch.	Slok	Meaning
sarira-vang-manobhih	18	15	with the body, speech, and mind
sarira-yatra	3	8	body maintenance
sarire	1	29	in the body
sarma	11	25	comfort
sarva	11	4	all
sarva kamebhyah	6	18	for all desirable objects
sarva-arambah	18	48	all undertakings
sarva-arambha-parityagi	12	16	who has renounced all initiative of action
sarva-arthan	18	32	all objects
sarva-ascaryamayam	11	11	abounding in wonder everywhere
sarva-bhavena	15	19	with whole being
sarva-bhrt	13	14	supporter of all
sarva-bhuta-asaya-sthitah	10	2	dwelling in the hearts of all beings
sarva-bhutanam	2	69	of all creatures
sarva-bhutani	6	29	in all creatures
sarva-bhutasthitam	6	31	abiding in all beings
sarva-bhutatm abhutatma	5	7	the self of the selves of all beings
sarva-bhute-hite	5	25	in the happiness of all beings
sarva-bhutesu	3	18	in all beings
sarva-dehinam	14	8	of all embodied beings
sarva-dharman	18	66	all duties
sarva-dukhanam	2	65	all sorrows

Sanskrit Word	Ch.	Slok	Meaning
sarva-durgani	18	58	all difficulties
sarva-dvarani	8	12	all passages
sarva-dvaresu	14	13	through all passages
sarva-gatah	2	24	omnipresent
sarvaghatam	3	15	to all-pervading
sarva-guhya-tamam	18	64	of utmost secrecy
sarvah	3	5	all
sarvah	8	18	all
sarva-harah	10	34	destroyer of all
sarvaih	15	15	through all
sarva-indriya-vivarjitam	13	14	devoid of all senses
sarva-jnana vimudhan	3	32	who are confused about all knowledge
sarva-karmanam	18	13	of all actions
sarva-karmani	3	26	all the duties
sarva-karmaphala-tyagam-kuru	12	11	give up the result of all work
sarva-kilbisaih	3	13	from all sins
sarva-ksetresu	13	2	in all the fields
sarva-loka-maheswaram	5	29	the great Lord of all the worlds
sarvam	2	17	all
sarvani	2	3	all
sarva-papaih	10	3	from all sins
sarva-papebhyah	18	66	from all sins

Sanskrit Word	Ch.	Slok	Meaning
sarvasah	1	18	in various ways
sarva-samkalpa-sannyasi	6	4	who has abandoned thought of everything
sarvasya	2	3	of all
sarvatah	2	46	all round
sarvatah-pani padam	13	13	which has hands and feet everywhere
sarvatah-srutimat	13	13	which has ears everywhere
sarvatha	6	31	whatever
sarvato-di-ptimantam	11	17	shining all around
sarvatoksi-siro-mukham	13	13	which has eyes, heads, and mouths everywhere
sarvatra	2	57	everywhere
sarvatragah	9	6	moving everywhere
sarvatragam	12	3	all-pervading
sarvatra-sama-darsanah	6	2	who sees everything in the same manner
sarva-vedesu	7	8	in all the Vedas
sarva-vit	15	19	omniscient
sarva-vrksanam	10	26	among all trees
sarva-yajanam	9	24	of all sacrifices
sarva-yonisu	14	4	from all wombs
sarve	1	6	all
sarvebhyah	4	36	among all
sarvendriya-guna-abhasam	13	14	shining with the activites of all senses
sarvesu	1	11	in all

Sanskrit Word	Ch.	Slok	Meaning
sasankah	11	39	the moon
sasvat	9	31	ever-lasting
sat	9	19	existence
satah	2	16	of the real, of the self
satatam	3	19	always
satatayuktah	12	1	being always devoted
satata-yuktanam	10	1	who are always devoted
sathavara-jangamam	13	26	moving or non-moving
sati	18	16	being
satkaramana-pujartham	17	18	for getting name, fame and being worshipped
satrau	12	18	towards an enemy
satruh	16	14	enemy
satrum	3	43	enemy
satrun	11	33	enemies
satrutve	6	6	hostile
satruvat	6	6	like an enemy
sattva-anurupa	17	3	in accordance with nature
sattvam	10	36	virtuous
sattva-samavistah	18	1	endowed with virtue
sattva-samsuddhih	16	1	mental purity
sattvastah	14	18	those who stick to sattva or virtue
sattvat	14	17	from virtue
sattva-vatam	10	36	of the virtuous persons
sattve	14	14	in virtue

Sanskrit Word	Ch.	Slok	Meaning
sattvikah	17	11	those with the sattva quality
sattvika-priyah	17	8	favourite of one endowed with sattva
sattviki	17	2	born of sattva
Satyakih	1	17	name of a warrior
satyam	10	4	truth
Saubhadrah	1	6	son of Subhadra - the wife of Arjuna
sauksmyat	13	32	because of its subtletly
Saumadatti	1	8	son of Somadatta
saumyam	11	51	serene
saumyatvam	17	16	gentleness
saumyavapuh	11	5	graceful form
savijnanam	7	2	together
savikaram	13	6	together with knowledge
savyasachin	11	33	name of Arjuna
senaninam	10	24	among commanders
senayoh	1	21	of thearmies
sevate	14	26	serves
sevaya	4	34	through service
Shaibyah	1	5	a king of the sibi tribe
Shankarah	10	23	an ephithet of Siva - God of destruction
shariram	4	21	bodily
shasi-surya-netram	11	19	having the sun and the moon as eyes

Sanskrit Word	Ch.	Slok	Meaning
shastra-bhrutam	10	31	among the wielders of weapons
shastram	15	2	the scriptures
shastrani	2	23	weapons
shastra-panayah	1	46	armed with weapons
shastra-sampate	1	2	discharge of weapons
shastra-vidhana uktam	16	24	as prescribed in the scriptures
shastra-vidhim	16	23	what is prescribed in the scriptures
shasva tam	10	12	eternal
shasvata-dharma gopta	11	18	protector of the eternal dharma
shasvatah	2	2	undying
shasvatah	1	43	eternal
shasvate	8	26	eternal
shasvatih	6	41	eternal
shatashah	11	5	in hundreds
shathah	18	28	deceitful
shaucham	13	7	cleanliness
shauryam	18	43	valour
Shikhandi	1	17	name of the charioteer on Pandava side. He was instrumental in the killing of the warrior Bhishma
shochati	12	7	grieves
shochitum	2	26	to grieve
shokam	2	28	sorrow

Sanskrit Word	Ch.	Slok	Meaning
shokasamvi-gnamanasah	1	47	with a mind filled with sorrow
shosayati	2	23	dries
shraddadhanah	6	37	with faith
shrnoti	2	29	hears
shrnu	2	39	listen
shrnuyat	18	71	may hear
shrnvan	5	8	hearing
shrnvatah	10	18	while hearing
shubha-asubham	2	57	good or bad
shubha-asubha-parityagi	12	17	who renounce good and bad
shubha-asubha-phalaih	9	28	which produce good and bad results
shubhan	18	71	the auspicious
shuchau	6	11	in a clean
shuchinam	6	41	of the pious
shudrah	9	32	sudras - one of the four castes; the service providers
shudranam	18	41	of the sudras
shudrasya	18	44	of the sudra
shuni	5	18	on a dog
shurah	1	4	heroes
shyalah	1	34	brothers-in-law
sidanti	1	28	become languid
siddhah	16	14	perfect
siddhanam	7	3	among the siddhas

Sanskrit Word	Ch.	Slok	Meaning
siddha-sanghah	11	36	groups of the siddhas
siddhau	4	22	in success
siddhaye	7	3	for the accomplishment
siddhi-asiddhyoh	2	48	by success and defeat
siddhih	4	12	succeeds
siddhim	3	4	fruition of actions
sikharinam	10	23	among the mountain peaks
simhanadam	1	12	lions roar
sirasa	11	14	with head
sisyah	2	7	disciple
sisyena	1	3	by disciple
sita-usna sukha-duhkha-dah	2	14	producers of cold, heat, pleasure and pain
sita-usna-sukha-duhkhesu	6	7	in the midst of cold, heat, joy and sorrow
Skandah	10	24	a war-god, chief of Gods-army
smaran	3	6	remembering
smarati	8	14	remembers
smrta	6	19	thought of
smrtah	17	23	regarded
smrtam	17	2	referred to
smrti-bhramsat	2	63	from failure of memory
smrtih	10	34	memory
smrti-vibhramah	2	63	failure of memory
snigdhah	13	7	nourishing
sodhum	5	23	withstand

Sanskrit Word	Ch.	Slok	Meaning
somah	15	13	the juice of the soma plant
somapah	9	2	those who drink the soma juice
sparsan	5	27	contacts
sparsanam	15	9	the organ of touch; skin
sprha	4	14	hankering
sprsan	5	8	touching
Sraddha	17	2	faith; a right by which the living offer the food to the manes and the departed. It is the yearly right performed by the children (sons) in rememberance of their departed parents
sraddham	7	21	faith
sraddhamayah	17	3	steeped in faith
sraddhavan	4	39	man of faith
sraddhavantah	3	31	faithfully
sraddha-virahitam	17	13	devoid of faith
sraddhya	6	37	with faith
sramsate	1	29	slips
sresthah	3	21	superior person
sreyah	1	31	superior
sreyan	3	35	superior to
srih	10	34	beauty
srimad	10	41	properous
srimatam	6	41	who prosper
sritah	9	12	possessed of

Sanskrit Word	Ch.	Slok	Meaning
srjami	4	7	I manifest
srjati	5	14	creates
sroryasi	18	58	will hear
srotasam	10	32	among rivers
srotavyasya	2	52	what has to be heard
srotradini	4	26	five senses like the eyes, ear etc
srotram	15	9	the ear
srstam	4	13	have been created
srstva	3	1	having created
srti	8	27	courses
srutam	18	72	heard
srutasya	2	52	what is heard
srutau	11	2	have been heard
srutavan	18	75	heard
sruti-paryanah	13	25	who are engaged in hearing
sruti-vi-pratipanna	2	53	confused by hearing the Vedas
srutva	2	29	after hearing
stabdhah	18	28	obstinate
stabdhah	16	17	those who are obstinate
stenah	3	12	theif
sthairyam	17	8	steadiness
sthanam	5	5	liberation
sthane	11	36	it is proper
sthanuh	2	24	stationary
sthapaya	1	21	fix

Sanskrit Word	Ch.	Slok	Meaning
sthapayitva	1	24	having fixed
sthasyati	2	53	will become
sthira-buddhih	5	2	man of steady intellect
sthirah	6	13	substantial
sthiram	6	11	steady
sthira-matih	12	19	steady minded
sthita-dhih	2	54	man of steady wisdom
sthitah	5	2	who is established
sthitah	5	19	are established
sthitam	5	19	established
sthitan	1	26	marshalled
sthita-prajhasya	2	54	of a man of steady wisdom
sthitau	1	14	stationed
sthitih	2	72	steadfastness
sthitim	6	33	continuance
sthitya	2	72	by being established
sthivarinam	10	25	of the immovables
strisu	1	41	of women
striyah	9	32	women
stutibhih	11	21	hymns
stuvanti	11	21	praise
suchah	16	5	grieve
suchih	12	16	the pure one
su-duracharah	9	3	a very wicked man
sudur-darsam	11	52	difficult to see
su-durlabhah	7	19	very rare

Sanskrit Word	Ch.	Slok	Meaning
suduskaram	6	34	extremely difficult
Sughosa mani-puspakau	1	16	two conchs named Sugosha and Manipushpaka
suhrda	1	26	friend
suhrdanmitraryu da	6	9	to a benefactor
suhrt	9	18	friend
sukha-duhkha-nam	13	2	of happiness and sorrow
sukha-duhkhe	2	38	happiness and sorrow
sukha-dukha sanjaih	15	5	known as happiness and sorrow
sukham	2	66	happiness
sukhani	1	31	pleasures
sukhasangena	14	6	through attachment to happiness
sukhasaya	14	27	of happiness
sukhe	14	9	to happiness
sukhena	6	28	easily
sukhesu	2	56	for happiness
sukhi	5	23	happy
sukhinah	1	37	happy
suklah	8	24	the bright fortnight
sukla-krsne	8	26	white and black
sukrta-duskrte	2	5	virtue and vice
sukrtam	5	15	virtue
sukrtasya	14	16	of good
sukrtinah	7	16	of noble deeds
suksmatvat	13	15	because of subtlety

Sanskrit Word	Ch.	Slok	Meaning
sulabhah	8	14	easy to attain
sunischitam	5	1	for certain
sura-ganah	10	2	neither the gods
suranam	2	8	over the gods
sura-sanghah	11	21	groups of gods
surendra-lokam	9	2	the world of the king of gods
suryah	15	6	the Sun
surya-sahastrasya	11	12	of one thousand suns
susukham	9	2	very easy
Suta-putrah	11	26	The name of Karna, a prominent Kaurava warrior; literal meaning is - son of charioteer
sutre	7	7	on a string
suvirudha-mulam	15	3	with roots well developed
suyate	9	1	produces
svabandvan	1	37	one's own relatives
svabavajam	18	42	natural
svabhavah	5	14	nature
svabhavaja	17	2	nature
svabhavajena	18	6	born of nature
svabhavaniyatan	18	47	as guided by one's nature
svabhava-prabhavaih	18	41	born from nature
sva-chaksusa	11	8	eye of yours
svadha	9	16	food offered to manes

Sanskrit Word	Ch.	Slok	Meaning
sva-dharmah	3	35	one's own duty
sva-dharmam	2	31	one's own duty
sva-dharme	3	35	in one's own duty
svadhya-jnana-yajnah	4	28	sacrifice through study and knowledge
svadhyaya-abhya-sanam	17	15	the practice of the mastery of the scriptures
svadhyayah	16	1	study of the Vedas
sva-janam	1	28	relatives
svakam	11	5	his own
sva-karma-nir atah	18	45	one devoted to ones own duty
svalpam	2	4	a little
svam	4	6	my own
svanusthitat	3	35	well performed
svapake	5	18	an outcaste
svapan	5	8	sleeping
svapnam	18	35	sleep
svarga-dwaram	2	32	heavenly gate
svarga-lokam	9	21	heavenly world
svargam	2	37	heaven
svarga-parah	2	43	with heaven as the goal
svargatim	9	2	heavenly goal
svasan	5	8	breathing
svasthah	14	24	tranquil
svasti	11	21	well
svasurah	1	34	fathers-in-law
svasuran	1	26	fathers-in-law

Sanskrit Word	Ch.	Slok	Meaning
sva-tejasa	11	19	your own brilliance
svaya	7	2	by their own
svayam	4	38	oneself
svena	18	6	by your own
svetaih	1	14	white
swam	6	13	at the tip
syakarmana	18	46	with ones duties
syam	3	24	shall be
syama	1	37	may be
syandane	1	14	in the chariot
syat	1	36	can be
syuh	9	32	born
taamasa-priyam	17	1	liked by people having the tamasik disposition
tada	1	2	at that time
tadanantaram	17	27	soon after that
tadartham	3	9	for that sake
tadarthiyam	17	27	meant for these
tadvat	2	7	in the same way
tadvidah	13	1	who are experts in this
tamah	10	11	darkness
tamasam	17	13	based on tamas
tamasi	14	13	in darkness
tamo dvaraih	16	22	doors to darkness, delusion
tannisthah	5	17	who are firm in that

Sanskrit Word	Ch.	Slok	Meaning
tanum	7	21	body
tapah	7	9	austerity
tapantam	11	19	heating up
tapasa	11	53	by austerity
tapyante	17	5	undertake
tasmat	1	37	therefore
tasmin	14	3	in that
tasya	1	12	of that
tasyam	2	69	in that
tat.bhava.bhavitah	8	6	concentrated in its thought
tatam	2	17	is pervaded
tat-buddhayah	5	17	those who have their wisdom concentrated in that
tat-para yanah	5	17	who have that as their ultimate goal
tatparah	4	39	who is devoted
tat-param	5	16	that supreme self
tat-prasadat	18	62	through His blessings
tatra	1	26	there
tattva-jnanartha darsanam	13	11	insight into the goal of the knowledge of Reality
tatva-darsibhih'	2	1	by the seers of Truth
tatva-dars'inah	4	3	who have realized the Truth
tatvam	18	1	the truth
tatva-vit	3	28	knower of Truth
tatvena	9	24	in reality

Sanskrit Word	Ch.	Slok	Meaning
tava	1	3	your
taya	2	44	with that
tejorasim	11	17	a mass of brightness
tisthati	3	5	resides
titiksasva	2	14	to bear
traigunya-visayah	2	45	related to the realm of the activities of three qualities - sattva, rajas and tamas
trailokya-rajyasya	1	35	for the kingdom of the three worlds, namely, the earth, the heaven and the intermediate region
trayam	16	21	by three
trayate	2	4	saves
tribhih	7	13	three
tridha	18	19	of three kinds
trin	14	2	three
trisu	3	22	in the three
trividhah	17	7	of three kinds
trividham	16	21	of three kinds
trptih	10	18	satisfaction
trsna-sanga samudabhvam	14	7	arising from hankering and attachment
tulya-ninda atma samstutih	14	24	to whom criticism and self-praise are the same; man of equi-poised disposition
tumulah	1	13	tremendous
tusnim	2	9	silent

Sanskrit Word	Ch.	Slok	Meaning
tustah	2	55	remains pleased
tustih	10	5	satisfaction
tusyati	6	2	one remains satisfied
tvadanyah	6	39	other than you
tvadanyena	1	47	by anyone other than you
tvattah	11	2	from you
tyajyam	18	3	should be renounced
tyaktum	18	11	to give up
tyaktva	1	33	by giving up
ubhe	2	5	both
ucchaihs'ravasam	10	27	the divine horse on which the king of gods - Indra rides; this horse was born from the milky ocean and associated with nectar
ucchistam	17	1	remnants of a meal
udaahrtam	13	6	spoken of
udbhavah	10	34	prosperity
uddharet	6	5	one should help
udvijate	12	15	disturbed
udvijet	5	2	dejected
udyamya	1	2	having taken
udyatah	1	45	prepared
ugrah	11	3	fierce, intense
ugra-karmanah	16	9	given to cruel deeds
ugram	11	2	terrible

Sanskrit Word	Ch.	Slok	Meaning
ugrarupah	11	31	of terrible form
uktah	1	24	is stated
ukta-h	2	18	are stated
uktam	11	1	stated
uktva	1	47	having stated
ulbena	3	38	the bag called the womb in which the child is placed; the cover inside mothers body
unmisan	5	9	opening
upaasate	9	14	take to contemplation
upaasritah	4	1	burdened with
upaasritya	14	2	by resorting to
upaavisat	1	47	sat down
upaayatah	6	36	through the means
upadrsta	13	22	the witness
upaiti	6	27	attains
upajayante	14	2	born
upajayate	2	62	arises
upalabhyate	15	3	perceived
upalipyate	13	32	defiled
upama	6	19	comparison, poetic speech of simile
upapadyate	2	3	justified
upapannam	2	32	which presents itself
uparamate	6	2	gets retreated
uparamet	6	25	one should abstain
uparatam	2	35	having refrained

Sanskrit Word	Ch.	Slok	Meaning
upasangamya	1	2	having approached
upasevate	15	9	enjoys
upavisya	6	12	sitting
upayanti	10	1	they attain
upetah	6	37	possessed
upetya	8	15	reaching
uragan	11	15	serpents
urdhavam	12	8	upwards
urdhvamulam	15	1	that which has its roots at the top
urjitam	10	41	vigorous
Ushanaa	10	37	Sukracharya- the master of the demons; he is also the author of the treatise on morals- niti and economics- artha shastra. He is the counter part of Bruhaspati who discharges the similar work for the Gods
ushmapah	11	22	a category of manes
usitva	6	41	residing there
uta	1	4	also
utkramantam	15	1	departing
utkramati	15	8	departs
utsadanartham	17	19	for destruction
utsadyante	1	43	are destroyed
uttamah	15	17	supreme
uttamam	4	3	the best
uttama-ngaih	11	27	with their heads

Sanskrit Word	Ch.	Slok	Meaning
Uttamaujah	1	6	a warrior of great skill and strength
uttamavidam	14	14	of those who know the noblest
utthita	11	12	to shine brilliantly
uttisha	2	3	awake
vaadinah	2	42	who declares
vaasaamsi	2	22	clothes
vachah	2	1	utterance
vachanam	1	2	utterance
vada	3	2	you tell me
vadah	10	32	dialectic
vadanaih	11	3	mouths
vadati	2	29	talks about
vahami	9	22	I arrange
vahnih	3	38	fire
Vainateyah	10	3	Garuda, son of Vinata
vairagyena	6	35	through non-attachment
vairinam	3	37	the enemy
vaisvanarah	15	14	fire in the stomach, which helps the digestion of food
vaisyah	9	32	vaisyas - trading community
vaisya-karma	18	44	duties of vaisyas
vajram	10	28	Divine weapon of lord Indra, Thunderbolt
vak	10	34	speech
vaksyami	7	2	I shall tell

Sanskrit Word	Ch.	Slok	Meaning
vaktrani	11	27	mouths
vaktum	10	16	to speak
vakyam	1	2	speech
vanijyam	18	44	cultivation, cattle rearing and commerce
vara	8	4	being
varnasankara karakaih	1	43	which causes the inter-mingling of castes and sets in impurity of the races
varna-sankarah	1	41	mixing of castes
varsam	9	4	rain
Varsneya	1	41	O, scion of the Vrsni dynasty; another name for Krishna
vartamanani	7	26	present
vartate	5	26	there is
varte	3	22	I continue
varteta	6	6	acts
varteyam	3	23	continue
vartma	3	23	path
Varuna	10	29	god of the waters
vasah	1	44	living
vasam	3	34	influence
vasat	9	8	under influence
Vasavah	11	22	Vasus; demi-gods of wealth
Vasavah	10	22	Indra- Indra is the Lord of Heaven
vase	2	61	under discipline

Sanskrit Word	Ch.	Slok	Meaning
vasi	5	13	man of self-discipline
Vasudevah	7	19	name of Krishna
Vasuki	10	28	King of serpents or the Nagas
vasyatmana	6	36	by one of disciplined mind
vayuh	2	67	the wind
veda	2	21	know
vedah	2	45	the Vedas
vedaih	11	53	through Vedas
vedanam	10	22	among the Vedas
veda-vada-ratah	2	42	who are absorbed in the wisdom of the Vedas
veda-vidah	8	11	those who know the Vedas
vedavit	15	1	versed in the Vedas
vede	15	18	in the Vedas
vedesu	2	46	regarding the Vedas
vedhyah	15	15	object to be known
vedhyam	9	17	object of knowledge
veditavyam	11	18	to be known
veditum	18	1	to be known
vegam	5	23	impulse
vepamanah	11	35	trembling
vepathuh	1	29	trembling
vetta	11	38	knower of all things
vettha	4	5	know
vetti	2	19	knows
vibhaktam	13	16	divided

Sanskrit Word	Ch.	Slok	Meaning
vibhaktesu	18	2	in the different things
vibhavasau	7	9	in the fire
vibhuh	5	15	the omnipresent
vibhuhnam	10	4	to manifestations
vibhum	10	12	the omnipresent
vibhuteh	10	4	of manifestations
vibhutibhih	10	16	manifestations
vibhutim	10	7	divine minifestations
vibhutimat	10	41	possessed of majesty
vichaksanah	18	2	the learned ones
vichalayet	3	29	should disturb
vichalyate	6	22	disturbed
vichetasah	9	12	senseless
vidadhami	7	21	I strengthen
vidheya-atma	2	64	self-controlled man
vidhi-hinam	17	13	contrary to the scriptures
vidhi-yate	2	44	established
vidhyam	10	17	I know
vidhyanam	10	32	among sciences
vidhyat	6	23	one should know
vidhya-vinaya sampanne	5	18	possessed of learning and humility
vidita-atmanam	5	26	who have known the self
vidvan	3	25	learned man
vigata-bhi	6	14	free from fear
vigatah	11	1	has departed

Sanskrit Word	Ch.	Slok	Meaning
vigata-iccha bhaya.krodhah	5	28	free from desire, fear and anger
vigata-jvarah	3	3	who is devoid of desire
vigatakalmasah	6	28	faultless
vigata-sprihah	2	56	devoid of mental fever
vigunah	11	1	defective
vihara-sayya-asana-bhojanesu	11	42	while at play or on bed or seated or at meals
vihaya	2	22	after discarding
vihitah	17	23	ordained
vijanatah	2	46	who knows the reality
vijanitah	2	19	know the self
vijaniyam	4	4	am I to know
vijayam	1	31	victory
vijita-indriyah	6	8	who has controlled his organs
vijitatma	5	7	controlled in body
vijnanam	18	42	wisdom
vijnana-sahitam	9	1	combined with experience
vijnatum	11	31	to know well
vijnaya	13	18	by understanding
vikampitum	2	31	to deviate
Vikarana	1	8	the third of the hundred sons of Dhrtarashtra
vikarmanah	4	17	about forbidden action
vikrantah	1	6	valiant
viksante	11	22	gaze
vilagna	11	27	sticking

Sanskrit Word	Ch.	Slok	Meaning
vimastarah	4	22	being free from enmity
vimohayati	3	4	deludes
vimoksaya	16	5	for liberation
vimoksyase	4	32	you will be liberated
vimrsya	18	63	thinking over
vimubha-atma	3	6	of deluded mind
vimuchya	18	53	having abandoned
vimu-dhabhavah	14	49	bewildered state
vimudhah	15	1	who are deluded
vimuhyati	2	72	becomes deluded
vimuktah	9	28	becoming free
vimuktah	15	5	who have been freed
vimunchati	18	35	abandons
vina	10	39	without
vinadhya	1	12	raised
vinangsyasi	18	58	you will be ruined
vinasah	6	4	ruin
vinasam	2	17	the destruction
vinasaya	4	8	destroying
vinasyati	4	4	is ruined
vinasyatsu	13	27	among the ruined
vindami	11	24	I get
vindate	5	4	gets
vindati	4	38	attains
vinischitaih	13	4	by the convincing
vinivartante	2	59	recede

Sanskrit Word	Ch.	Slok	Meaning
viniyamya	6	24	controlling
viniyatam	6	18	controlled
viparitam	18	15	opposite
viparitan	18	32	opposed to
vipari-vartate	9	1	revolves
viparrta-ni	1	3	adverse
vipaschritah	2	6	of an intelligent
Viratah	1	4	name of the king
viryavan	1	5	valiant
vis is yate	3	7	excels
visadam	18	35	despair
visadi	18	28	one who is in despair
visalam	9	21	vast
visam	18	37	poison
visame	2	2	in this hour of peril
visanti	14	11	enter
visargah	8	3	offerings
visate	18	55	enters
visaya pravalah	15	2	with sense objects for their shoots
visayah	2	59	objects of senses
visaya-indriya-samyogat	18	38	originating from the organs and their objects
visayan	2	62	on objects of senses
visidan	1	27	in despair
visidendam	13	17	who was in despair

Sanskrit Word	Ch.	Slok	Meaning
visistah	1	7	foremost
vismaya-avistah	11	14	wonderstruck
vismayah	18	77	with wonder
vismitah	11	22	being struck with wonder
Visnuh	10	21	Vishnu - The God who preserves the universe
visrjami	9	7	send forth
visrjan	5	9	releasing
visrjya	1	47	casting aside
vistabhya	10	42	supporting
vistaram	13	3	spreading
vistarasah	11	2	in detail
vistarasya	10	19	of detail
vistarena	10	18	in detail
vistitam	16	17	seated
visuddhatma	5	7	of pure mind
visuddhaya	18	51	pure
Visvam	11	19	Universal
Visvamurte	11	46	O, you of universal form
Visvarupa	11	16	O, universal person
visvatomukham	9	15	facing many directions
Visve	11	22	Visva-devas consisting of Rudras and other gods
visveswara	11	16	O, Lord of the universe
vita-ra gah	8	11	free from attachment

Sanskrit Word	Ch.	Slok	Meaning
vita-raga-bhaya-krodhah	2	56	free from attachment, fear and anger
vitatah	4	32	spread
vivasvan	4	1	the sun
vivasvatah	4	4	of vivasyan, the sun
vivasvate	4	1	to vivasvan, the sun
vivatomukhah	10	33	with faces everywhere
vividhah	17	25	many
vividhaih	13	4	by many kinds of
vivikta-desa sevitvam	13	1	resort to quiet places
vivikta-sevi	18	52	one who resorts to a quiet place
vivrdd ham	14	11	increased
vivrddhe	14	12	increases
vraja	18	66	take
vrajeta	2	54	move about
Vrikrodarah	1	15	Bhima, one of the Pandavas
vrjinam	4	36	sin
Vrsninam	10	37	Vrsni race to which Krishna belonged
vyadarayat	1	19	pierced
vyaharan	8	1	while speaking
vyaipya	10	16	permeating
vyaktamadhyani	2	28	manifest in the middle
vyaktim	7	24	glory
vyapasritya	9	32	by taking refuge

Sanskrit Word	Ch.	Slok	Meaning
vyaptam	11	2	is permeated
Vyasa-prasadat	18	75	through Vyasas favour
vyatha	11	49	fear
vyathayanti	2	15	disturb
vyathisthah	11	34	be afraid
vyatitani	4	5	have passed
vyatitansyati	2	52	will cross over
vyatta-ananam	11	24	open-mouthed
vyavasayah	10	36	determination
vyavasayatmika	2	41	single determination
vyavasitah	9	3	determined
vyavasthitan	1	2	standing arrayed
vyavasthitau	3	34	seated
vyavastitah	1	45	prepared
vyktayah	8	18	manifested things
vymisrena	3	2	conflicting
vyudasya	18	51	removing
vyudham	1	2	in battle order
vyudham	1	3	battle array
yabhih	10	16	through which
yacchraddhah	17	3	which is the faith of the individual
yada	2	52	when
yadasam	10	29	of the deities in water
Yadava	11	41	name of Krishna

Sanskrit Word	Ch.	Slok	Meaning
yadi	1	38	if
yadrccha-labha santustah	4	22	pleased with what comes unexpected
yadrcchaya	2	32	unexpected
yadrk	13	3	how it is
yadvat	2	7	as
yagnah	4	32	sacrifices
yagna-vidah	4	3	those who know about sacrifice
yah	14	4	whatever
yajantah	9	15	by glorifying
yajante	9	23	they worship
yajha-bavitah	3	12	being nurtured by sacrifices
yajna.sista-asinah	3	13	those who consume the remnants of sacrifices
yajna-dana-tapah kriyah	17	24	the act of sacrifice, charity and austerity
yajnaih	9	2	through sacrifice
yajna-ksapita kalmasah	4	3	have their sins destroyed by the performance of the sacrifices
yajnam	4	25	sacrifice
yajnanam	10	25	among sacrifices
yajnarthat	3	9	meant for sacrifice
yajna-sista-amrta bhujah	4	31	those who consume the nectar remaining after sacrifice
yajnat	3	14	from sacrifice

Sanskrit Word	Ch.	Slok	Meaning
yajna-tapah kriyah	17	25	works of sacrifice and austerity
yajna-tapasam	5	29	of sacrifices and austerities
yajnaya	4	23	for a sacrifice
yajnena	9	2	in sacrifice
yajnena	4	25	by sacrifice
yajuh	9	17	Yajur Veda
yaksa-raksasam	10	23	among the Yaksas and goblins
yaksye	16	15	I shall perform sacrifice
yam	2	15	whom
yam	2	42	whichever
Yamah	10	29	King of death
yanti	3	33	follow
yantra-arudhani	18	61	hoisted on a machine
yashah	10	5	fame
yasmat	12	15	owing to which
yasmin	6	22	in which
yasya	2	61	whose
yasyam	2	69	in which
yasyasi	2	35	will tell
yata atmanah	5	25	whose organs are controlled
yata-atma	12	14	self-controlled
yata-atmavan	12	11	whose mind is controlled
yata-cetasam	5	26	whose internal organs are under control
yata-chitta-atma	4	21	whose body and mind are controlled

Sanskrit Word	Ch.	Slok	Meaning
yata-chitta-indriya kryah	6	12	controlling the actions of the mind and senses
yata-chittasya	6	19	whose mind is controlled
yatah	6	26	because of
yatamanah	12	11	applying himself
yatantah	9	14	striving
yatanti	7	29	strive
yatata	6	36	by one who tries
yatatah	2	6	while trying earnestly
yatate	6	43	he strives
yatati	7	3	efforts
yata-vak-kaya-ma-nasah	8	52	whose speech body and mind are controlled
yatayah	4	28	ascetics
yata-yamam	17	1	food cooked three hours earlier, that is, stale food, insipid, lost of taste
yatendriya mano-buddhih	5	28	who has controlled his organs mind and intellect
yatha	2	13	in which manner
yathabhagam	1	11	in different directions
yathavat	18	19	as they are
yatinam	5	26	to the monks
yatra	6	2	where
yavan	2	46	what I am
yavat	1	22	whatever
Yaya	2	39	with which

Sanskrit Word	Ch.	Slok	Meaning
yena	2	17	by which
yesam	1	32	in the case of those
yoddhavyam	1	22	must be fought
yoddhukaman	1	22	who are intending to fight
yodha mukhyaih	11	26	senior commanders
yodha-veeraan	11	34	brave warriors
yodhah	11	32	warriors
yoga sanjnitam	6	23	what is known as yoga
yoga sevaya	6	2	through the practice of yoga
yoga-arudhah	6	4	established in yoga
yoga-arudhasya	6	3	when he has reached yoga
yoga-balena	8	1	with the strength of yoga
yoga-brastah	6	41	one who has fallen from yoga
yogadharanam	8	12	Practice of Yoga
yogaih	5	5	by the yogis
yogakshemam	9	22	welfare and security
yogam	2	53	yoga (see under yogadharanam)
yoga-mayasamavrtah	7	25	being veiled by creative power
yoga-samsiddhin	6	37	perfection in yoga
yoga-sannyasta karmanam	4	41	one who has given up action through yoga
yoga-sarisiddhat	4	38	one who has attained perfection through yoga
yogasthali	2	48	by being settled in yoga
yogasya	6	44	of yoga

Sanskrit Word	Ch.	Slok	Meaning
yogat	6	37	from yoga
yoga-vittamah	12	1	those who are well versed in yoga
yoga-yajnah	4	28	those who perform sacrifices through yoga
yoga-yukta-atma	6	29	whose mind is self absorbed in yoga
yoga-yuktah	5	6	firmness in yoga
yogena	10	7	with yoga
Yogesvarah	18	78	Lord of Yoga
Yogesvarat	18	75	from the Lord of Yoga
Yogeswarah	11	4	O Lord of Yoga
yogi	5	24	a man of concentrated mind
yoginam	6	27	to this yogi
yoktavyah	6	23	has to be practised
yonih	14	3	womb
yotsyamanan	1	23	those who have the intention to fight
youvanam	2	13	youth
yuddha visaradhah	1	9	proficient in battle
yuddham	2	32	battle
yuddhaya	2	37	for fighting
yuddhyasva	2	18	engage in battle
Yudhamanyu	1	6	name of a great warrior
yudhi	1	4	in battle
Yudhisthirah	1	16	the eldest of the five sons of Pandu

Sanskrit Word	Ch.	Slok	Meaning
yugapat	11	12	simultaneously
yuga-sahasra-antam	8	17	which ends in a thousand yugas
yuge	4	8	Yuga means a historical period
yujyasva	2	38	you engage in battle
yukta-ahara viharasya	6	17	of one who is restrained in his eating and movements
yukta-chestasya	6	17	of one who is moderate in his action
yukta-chetasah	7	3	of disciplined minds
yuktaih	17	17	by those who are self controlled
yukta-svapna avabodhasya	6	17	of one who is moderate in sleep and in wakefulness
yukta-tamah	12	2	the most devoted yogis
Yuktatma	7	18	with a firm mind
yunjan	6	15	concentrating
yunjatah	6	19	who is engaged in
yunjita	6	1	should concentrate
yunjyat	6	12	should concentrate
yunkte	1	14	yoked
yuyutsavah	1	1	eager for battle
yuyutsum	1	28	eager to fight

• • •